Drama at the Heart of the Second

Drama at the Heart of the Secondary School provides a rationale for the curricular centrality of drama together with rich and detailed examples of cross-phase thematic projects which are drama-led, but which promote learning across a wide range of curriculum areas, from the humanities and other arts, to English and literacy, science and PSHE.

Each unit explores relevant and stimulating themes and topics that will engage the students, promote empathy, pose questions, and produce creative responses. Starting from relatively simple beginnings, the drama is structured in layers of increasing sophistication and complexity. Each layer adds another dimension to the potential learning opportunities available across a wide range of curriculum areas and suitable for learners of varying experience and ability. A wide range of curriculum areas of enquiry are referenced, and each unit offers unique ways of student learning designed to encourage excellent drama skills as well as embracing the 'learning to learn', Citizenship and PSHE agendas that are fundamental to good teaching and learning.

Including downloadable resources suitable for student handouts at www.routledge.com/9780415572064, the book features:

- lists of dramatic techniques and keywords
- cross curricular connections and ideas highlighted in the text
- opportunities to address RSA 'Opening Minds' competencies and PLT skills
- examples of curriculum models suitable for thematic work
- an outline of the principles of assessment for each unit.

This accessible and practical textbook is essential for trainee and practising teachers interested in using drama to facilitate thematic, cross-curricular work in the classroom.

John Rainer is Academic Division Leader for Arts, Humanities and Language Education within the Institute of Education, Manchester Metropolitan University. He is also the Course Co-ordinator for PGCE Drama.

Martin Lewis is Director of Arts at Kingsbridge Community College.

Drama at the Heart of the Secondary School

Projects to promote authentic learning

John Rainer and Martin Lewis

Routledge
Taylor & Francis Group

LONDON AND NEW YORK

First published 2012
by Routledge
2 Park Square, Milton Park, Abingdon, Oxon OX14 4RN

Simultaneously published in the USA and Canada
by Routledge
711 Third Avenue, New York, NY 10017

Routledge is an imprint of the Taylor & Francis Group, an informa business

British Library Cataloguing in Publication Data
A catalogue record for this book is available from the British Library

Library of Congress Cataloging in Publication Data
   Drama at the heart of the secondary school : projects to promote authentic learning / John
   Rainer and Martin Lewis.
      p. cm.
   Includes bibliographical references.
   1. Acting—Study and teaching (secondary).   2. Drama in education.   I. Lewis, Martin,
   1966– II. Title.
   PN2075.R35 2012
   792.02'80712—dc23   2011028077

ISBN: 978-0-415-57205-7 (hbk)
ISBN: 978-0-415-57206-4 (pbk)
ISBN: 978-0-203-14130-4 (ebk)

Typeset in Celeste
by RefineCatch Limited, Bungay, Suffolk

Printed and bound in Great Britain by the MPG Books Group

Contents

Figures

Figures

Tables

Acknowledgements

Figures

Figure 1.1, Image from *Babes in the Wood*, by Randolph Caldecott, Reproduced with permission of Pook Press (2010). Figure 1.2 Birth tokens, Reproduced with permission of the Thomas Coram Foundation for Children (Coram)/London Metropolitan Archives. Figure 4.1, Sir George Clausen, Bird Scaring: March, with special thanks to the Harris Museum in Preston. Figures 4.2 and 4.3, Watercress seller and chimney sweep, reproduced with permission of Mary Evans Picture Library. Figure 4.4, mining images, thanks to Beamish, The North of England Open Air Museum. Figure 5.1, Greek bowl depicting Helios, © Araldo de Luca/CORBIS. Figure 6.1, Plague scenes, with special thanks to the Museum of London. Figure 6.3, Woodcut depicting Londoners fleeing from the plague, © Historical Picture Archive/CORBIS. Figure 6.4, Plague house, with special thanks to Dr Neil Clifton. Figures 6.5, 6.6, 6.8 and 6.9, Plague window, with special thanks to Philip Wright. Figure 6.7, Eyam Church, with special thanks to Alan Fleming. Images from 'Red Shoes', Reproduced with permission of Mandy Coe http://www.mandycoe.com. Figure 8.1, Lizzie Borden images, Collection of Fall River Historical Society. Figure 8.2, Image from 'suck-a-thumb', in *Struwwelpeter*, by Heinrich Hoffman, Reproduced with permission of Dover Publications Inc. (1995). Figure 9.1, Young refugee from Nazi Germany, Reproduced with permission of the Manchester Jewish Museum.

Text

Text from *Babes in the Wood*, by Randolph Caldecott, Reproduced with permission of Pook Press (2010). *Caucasian Chalk Circle*, © Bertolt Brecht and Methuen Drama, an imprint of Bloomsbury Publishing Plc. *The Testimony of Patience Kershaw*, Reproduced with permission of The English Folk, Dance and Song Society. Text from Save the Children website, with special thanks to http://www.savethechildren.org.uk. *A Journal of the Plague Year*, by Daniel Defoe, Reproduced with permission of Dover Publications Inc. (2001). Text from 'suck-a-thumb', in *Struwwelpeter*, by Heinrich

Acknowledgements

Hoffman, Reproduced with permission of Dover Publications Inc. (1995). Text from 'A Memory of Lizzie', in *Drama Anthologies: Sepia and Song*, David Foxton, 978–0174324096, first published in 1994, Reproduced with the permission of Nelson Thornes Ltd on behalf of David Foxton.

'Kindertransport', Diane Samuels, Reproduced with permission of Nick Hern Books Ltd (2008). 'Refugee Blues', *Collected Works*, Copyright © 1976, 1991, The Estate of W. H. Auden, granted by permission of The Wylie Agency (UK) Ltd.

Introduction

This book is aimed at all secondary school teachers who are keen to use drama to provide a framework for creative, thematic and cross-curricular learning that is *authentic* – rooted in real-world issues, dilemmas and narratives.

It has long been recognized that drama can provide a rich context for such work, but in recent times an overcrowded, assessment-driven and fragmented curriculum has tended to devalue arts-led integrated teaching and learning. The time is now right to re-establish drama at the centre of a creative, thematic curriculum, benefiting both learners and teachers.

Put simply, the book aims to provide a rationale for the curricular centrality of drama, together with rich and detailed examples of cross-phase thematic projects which are drama-led, but which promote learning across a wide range of curriculum areas – notably the humanities and other arts, but also English and literacy, Science and Personal Social and Health Education. Throughout, the emphasis will be on providing an authentic, if fictional, context for cross-curricular explorations, without sacrificing the integrity or aesthetic quality of the drama work itself.

Although the book is primarily a practical guide to teaching in this way, in passing we will also explore more theoretical questions and issues raised by this approach. For instance, we will attempt to clarify misunderstood concepts at the centre of both drama and humanities education such as empathy and engagement; we will also attempt to avoid some of the pitfalls of previous understandings of thematic (or 'project') based approaches, and offer some thoughts on the importance of flexible approaches to the assessment of integrated learning which are learner-centred and fit for purpose.

Authentic learning

In the real world of lived experience, human beings do not learn in 50-minute periods divided into convenient categories called subjects. Our interaction with the world is seamless, integrated and free flowing, as we move from one activity or area of interest to another. In terms of the school curriculum, a familiar, but artificial hierarchy of atomized subjects stubbornly persists as an organizing principle in the vast majority of schools and colleges. Organizing learning in this way may have many advantages, but it often mitigates against students' ability to engage with the world of learning in a contextualized, organic and *authentic* manner.

In schools, the notion of relaxing, or even disbanding, these artificial categories of organizing learning in order to make students' experience more authentic has gone in and out of fashion – and political policy-making – over the last 60 years or so. One of the authors of this book, brought up in the 1960s and 1970s in the English midlands, attended a primary school organized around 'topic work', and a state 'progressive' secondary school[1] organized around a personalized and largely integrated curriculum. Later, as a member of a local authority performing arts advisory team in the 1980s,[2] he helped to deliver an *entitlement curriculum* based around areas of experience – not subjects – to the clusters of schools within the education authority. More recently in England and Wales, national curriculum reforms under the Blair Government – giving less emphasis to traditional subject-based approaches – created a resurgence of interest in exploring integrated and authentic means of curriculum organization and delivery. These innovations were attempts to create a curriculum more suited to the needs of twenty-first century learners than the previous iterations of the 1988 National Curriculum – which was noteworthy, perhaps, only due to its astounding similarity to the curriculum proposed in England at the turn of the twentieth century.[3]

In England, the Coalition Government elected in 2010 appears determined to return to a rigidly hierarchical school curriculum based on 'traditional subjects' once more – which to us seems, at best, nostalgic, and at worst, dangerously irrelevant.[4] Nevertheless, in schools faced with the challenge of educating students for an unknown future, the search for authenticity and relevance will continue.[5]

Constructivism and learning

Constructivist views free curriculum designers from the linear assumption of focusing on 'basics first' as the primary strategy for promoting learning. The instructional design process is expanded to explore a 'global view' before focusing in on 'local' details … Learners assume increasingly more control over the sequence in which they want to engage their learning and are free to explore the various local details of the topic. They can build their own mental frameworks in ways that are natural to them, unencumbered by a superimposed logical sequence.[6]

Based on the ideas of Piaget, and elaborated by Vygotsky, Bruner (in the form of *social* constructivism) and many others, constructivism suggests that learners *construct* knowledge and meaning out of their experiences.

One implication of constructivist theory is that didactic approaches to pedagogy should be abandoned in favour of more facilitative approaches. In addition, it emphasizes the social context of learning, seeing it as an active, social and collaborative process. It also sees the relationship between teacher and student as vital as they strive *together* to create meaning and understanding. Crucially, constructivist approaches stress the importance of context, in that *knowledge should not be divided into different subjects or compartments, but should be discovered as an integrated whole:*[7] in short, that learning should be a journey of co-discovery between teachers and students, and should be *authentic.*

Influenced by the ideas of constructivism, from the 1990s onwards academics and teachers began to codify pedagogic approaches that attempt to bring more *authenticity* to learning and teaching in schools, believing that this approach is more in tune with the needs of learners in the twenty-first century, and there have been a number of initiatives by various bodies, in the UK – and elsewhere – designed to bring more relevance to the curriculum. For instance, the Royal Society for the Arts' (RSA) competence-based *Opening Minds* initiative has proved influential in British schools, and its aims are certainly consonant with the pedagogic thrust of this publication:

> RSA Opening Minds promotes innovative and integrated ways of thinking about education and the curriculum. Teachers design and develop a curriculum for their own schools based round the development of five key competences:
>
> 1 Citizenship
> 2 Learning
> 3 Managing information
> 4 Relating to people
> 5 Managing situations
>
> A competence based approach enables students not just to acquire subject knowledge but to understand, use and apply it within the context of their wider learning and life. It also offers students a more holistic and coherent way of learning which allows them to make connections and apply knowledge across different subject areas.[8]

Other initiatives include the *Studio Schools* movement,[9] *Whole Education*[10] and the *Campaign for Learning;*[11] many of these initiatives seem to share similar principles – those of *authentic learning.*

Characteristics of authentic learning

Authentic Learning has several key characteristics:

- Learning is centred on authentic tasks that are of interest to the learners.
- Students are engaged in exploration and inquiry.
- Learning is interdisciplinary.
- Learning is closely connected to the world beyond the walls of the classroom.
- Students become engaged in complex tasks and higher-order thinking skills, such as analyzing, synthesizing, designing, manipulating and evaluating information.

- Students produce a product that can be shared with an audience outside the classroom.

- Learning is student driven with teachers, parents, and outside experts all assisting/coaching in the learning process.

- Learners employ scaffolding techniques.

- Students have opportunities for social discourse.

- Ample resources are available.[12]

In practice, despite its obvious appeal, organizing learning according to these principles may create practical difficulties; crafting authentic, real-world learning opportunities on a large scale across a wide curriculum would clearly present logistical and organizational problems beyond the scope of many schools. Perhaps for this reason, proponents are keen to stress that authenticity is a matter of *degree*:

> It is important to remember that authenticity does not mean you have to take students to the Louvre to learn about art, but that each lesson plan should subtly increase the amount of authenticity involved in the tasks. For example, tasks can fall on a continuum of authenticity where memorizing facts about paintings would be less authentic than visiting a web site that has a guided tour. But the guided tour is less authentic than actually visiting the museum. Schools should aim to make student experiences as authentic as possible to what happens in real life, and in doing so should provide support for the students to be reflective and to learn.[13]

Not surprisingly, the same author looks to technological solutions to this issue:

> Technology offers great advantages for authentic environments that were not available before. Technology can provide scaffolds for the students, and can allow students access to tools not normally encountered in schools.[14]

Readers will no doubt already be familiar with interesting examples of schools using technology in various ways – notably through online databases and interactive DVDs – to bring authentic learning environments into the classroom. In the near future the 'digital natives'[15] currently attending primary and secondary schools will expect technology of this kind to be ubiquitous and embedded in all learning programmes, and there are already schools where all pupils have access to a wide range of learning contexts through hand-held devices linked wirelessly.[16] Used imaginatively, ICT is clearly a powerful tool in making learning interactive and more authentic.

Authentic learning and drama

> (T)here are many practical, logistical, and political reasons why schools are limited in placing learners in realistic contexts . . . Even if politics and/or resources prevent authentic instruction, the use of simulations and role-playing can be substituted. Whatever approach is used to promote authentic teaching and learning, it is important to remember this: The

more authentic it feels to the learner, the better the results and the associated transfer of learning are likely to be.[17]

In our own work we have become conscious of how the use of drama – often in combination with ICT – can bring authentic cross-curricular learning into the classroom in very powerful ways. Experienced drama practitioners confronted with the 'key principles' of authentic learning may note how similar many of them are to the principles that underpin their own pedagogy. In their book, *Real Players? Drama, Technology and Education*[18] John Carroll, Michael Anderson and David Cameron provide case studies of how schools have utilized interactive online technologies to transform their teaching of drama and theatre. As Giuliana Dettori comments in her review of the book:[19]

> Live and mediated aspects should not be separate or in competition with each other—but articulated and integrated, giving rise to relevant forms of mixed experiences. Without this, we risk losing the interest of the younger generations, after all; they feel equally at ease with both the real and the virtual, and can be considered 'digital natives', having grown up in a technological world.

However, it is clearly a paradox that a pedagogy rooted in 'learning through imagined experience'[20] can add an authentic edge to teaching and learning which enthuses learners, motivating them to work beyond their teachers' expectations. Using a dramatic frame to structure learning, as has already been suggested, can satisfy many of the conditions of authenticity, but can often do so within a safe 'no penalty zone'[21] within which students can respond creatively to tasks without fear of failure. Using fictional, imagined, contexts to learn about the world brings authenticity to the classroom whilst avoiding the messy logistical problems of 'real' experience; the paradox is that whilst the context within which learning takes place is fictional, the learning motivated through students' engagement with those contexts is very real.

Mantle of the Expert

> You're not really at school. I'm interested in it because it seems like it's serious and really real.[22]

In the UK there has been a recent resurgence of interest in *Mantle of the Expert*, a role-based 'inquiry-teaching' methodology first devised by Dorothy Heathcote in the 1980s. In *Mantle of the Expert*, 'normal' classroom relationships are temporarily suspended; students are endowed with a particular expertise through the role they assume in the drama, and their expertise is developed as they collaborate in running a fictional enterprise or agency of some kind – behaving *as if* they are a group of experts responsible for completing tasks on behalf of *fictional* others. The teacher also operates in role, but crucially in this method of teaching, the expertise that is granted to the students is denied to the teacher. The teacher works alongside the students, but normally assumes a collaborative and facilitative role designed to enable them to co-operate to complete their tasks effectively – and to provoke reflection and challenge them when necessary.

In *Mantle of the Expert* students are therefore presented with a teacher who 'knows less than they do', forcing them to rely upon their own resources to complete the sometimes very complex – but always 'authentic' – tasks demanded by the fictional situation. Although in our experience *Mantle of the Expert* can become rather formulaic,[23] applied flexibly, this structure can bring authenticity to seemingly mundane tasks, and can have profound effects on student motivation. Many of the teaching units in this book rely upon the fundamental but temporary suspension in teacher/ student relationship that results from using drama in this way. One real advantage of this way of working is that open-ended tasks – often outwardly similar to everyday classroom activities – are motivated by the dramatic context; students see their responsibilities through with concern and pride in their work because the *drama* demands it, not the teacher!

Integrated learning and assessment

One criticism of thematic cross-curricular approaches to teaching and learning relates to the potential difficulties of assessing what has been learnt. This is particularly the case within a school system – such as that current in the UK – which is literally driven by assessment; where on a 'macro level' schools compete with each other in league tables compiled on the basis of student attainment as measured in seemingly arbitrary clusters of favoured subjects[24] – and where, in the classroom, teachers are required to go through the rituals – familiar to all who have visited British schools in the last 10 years or so – demanded of the *tripartite* lesson: 'learning objectives' outlined at beginning of the lesson, followed by activities where students demonstrate what skills and knowledge they have acquired during the lesson, concluded with a 'plenary' session, designed to review what has been learnt. Within this context – where learning is often seen in terms of a series of short-term objectives to be 'delivered' in a single lesson, is acquired and assessed according to a simplistic 'input–output' model, and is largely based on propositional knowledge or simple skills which can be easily tested – there may be some who reject the premise on which the model of teaching advocated in this book is based as 'woolly' or lacking in rigour.

However, this book is fundamentally about an approach to teaching rooted in the arts. A core belief – following the American arts educationalist Elliot Eisner[25] – is that at least some of what is learnt when students engage in arts activities should be *discovered in the process*. Many of the units in this book are structured using 'problem-based' approaches; by definition, if the problem is 'authentic', and the teacher is receptive to creative, risk-taking responses, problem-based structures demand a much more flexible and open approach to assessment: in exploring solutions to 'real' problems students will often be led into rich, but unpredictable, avenues of learning.

There is a growing, if far from universal, impatience with student assessment that addresses chiefly facts and basic skills, leaving thoughtfulness, imagination and pursuit untapped.[26]

Perhaps unsurprisingly, alongside the drive for a more authentic pedagogy have come calls for more authentic assessment methods.

The principles of authentic assessment are straightforward:

- Students should be given authentic, context-based tasks that give opportunities to show the application of knowledge, skills and understanding *through performance.*

- Students should be assessed on their abilities to **do things** in authentic settings, not just to know things or demonstrate de-contextualized skills.

- Students should understand (or be involved in negotiating) the criteria on which they are to be assessed, and should have a clear idea of the success criteria for a particular task.

- Students should be able to set themselves clear targets for improvement as a result of the process.[27]

However, transforming the curriculum and pedagogy to make it more authentic for learners will come to naught if assessment techniques default to the familiar, leading to *valuing what is assessed* rather than *assessing what is of value*:

> After all, what is the use of adopting loftier goals for yourself and your students if you continue to use multiple-choice tests that seek the 'right' answer, capturing only the lower-level knowledge that is easiest to measure? Rather than relying on a single assessment method, instructors who adopt authentic learning methods must analyze multiple forms of evidence to measure student performance, including observations of student engagement and artifacts produced in the process of completing tasks.[28]

In practice, applying the principles of authentic assessment might mean adopting 'portfolio' and performance-led assessment, where students play an active part in compiling what they believe provides evidence of learning over a whole project, and where use is made of peer and self-assessment to set clear targets for future learning.

Interestingly enough, in recent years in the UK some emphasis has been given to more student-centred and formative means of assessment – in the form of 'Assessment for Learning' (AfL).[29] However, this has worked in tension with the simultaneous demand to provide levelled summative assessments for all students at regular intervals. In drama, at least, this has resulted in some distortion as teachers, often faced with the task of assigning 'levels' to literally hundreds of students, base their teaching around that which is most easily assessed:

> (E)ducation has focused for too long on inculcating and assessing those cognitive skills that are relatively easy to acquire – remembering, understanding, and applying – rather

than the arguably more important skills of analyzing, evaluating, and creating. Moreover, in developing these lower-order thinking skills, educators have largely ignored the other major learning domains, particularly the conative, which determines whether a student has the necessary will, desire, commitment, mental energy, and self-determination to actually perform at the highest disciplinary standards. By engaging students in issues of concern to them … authentic learning awakens in learners the confidence to act.[30]

Social and moral learning

Learning also takes place within a social and ethical context. We believe that artists have a social responsibility and teachers, likewise, should be concerned that their students are engaging fully with the social world. Although the teaching units in the book are driven by significant content designed to provide the necessary engagement with authentic 'real-world' experience, we are less concerned with teaching students propositional knowledge about the learning contexts than facilitating an open-ended exploration of the material. Through this engagement, students acquire useful skills and understanding about the social world, and are able to enter into the moral, political and ethical issues raised by the material in such a way that their own beliefs are questioned and their values clarified. Drama – as writers such as Jo Winston[31] remind us – has a particular contribution to make to social learning of this kind: it can act as a crucible within which human actions, and the consequences of those actions, can be examined – and the students' own responses to the issues can be tested out in the safety provided by a fictional enactment.

Skills, understanding and values

Students engaging with the units in this book will also learn much about the art form of drama – its conventions, concepts and forms – and will develop skills necessary to construct and perform effective drama of their own. At the same time they will learn about the particular lesson content which provides a context for their dramatic explorations. For instance, in unit one, students will have opportunities to learn about aspects of eighteenth century social history through the story of Thomas Coram and his Foundling Hospital. However, our primary intention is not to teach historical dates and facts – although these may well be acquired through engaging with the work. Rather, we concentrate on the 'gaps' in history; the *liminal* areas 'between the facts' which deal with human motivation, feeling, moral choices and actions; this, we believe, is where drama is especially efficacious, and we hope that we follow in a long tradition of socially-committed theatre artists and teachers when we deal with historical and 'social' material in this way.

History, empathy and learning

This approach does, however, sometimes lead us to engage with some slippery concepts – such as *empathy*. Professor Simon Baron-Cohen, writing from a psychological perspective, suggests empathy has two elements:

> *Empathy is our ability to identify what someone else is thinking or feeling and to respond to those thoughts and feelings with an appropriate emotion.*[32]

Many might agree that inviting school students to imagine and feel what is going on 'inside' other human beings is a positive, perhaps crucial, process in a world where media accounts highlighting the consequences of lack of empathy and compassion for others are ubiquitous. However, encouraging empathy as part of the process of historical enquiry has long been contentious within the history teaching and academic community. Objections to encouraging empathetic responses in students have ranged from the complaint that the knowledge and content of history was being 'dumbed down' with 'soft' skills seemingly outside of the domain of rigorous evidence,[33] to concerns about with whom students might be empathizing,[34] to a postmodern critique that in encouraging empathy we may be privileging our contemporary understandings and ways of thinking and imposing them on the past.[35] Nevertheless, the use of role-play in history lessons is commonplace, and many history teachers would testify as to its educational worth.[36] For teachers from a drama background some interesting issues are raised in exploring historical material in this way; are we most concerned with history – or drama outcomes? Is it possible to facilitate lessons that are 'good drama' as well as 'good history'?

For us, all historical enactment, no matter how far it is based on evidence, is *fiction* – or, at best, fictionalized accounts of real events: it can only be drama *based on* history, not history itself. Sometimes the work that emerges might be good history, in the sense that students have used their imagination to try to gain some insight into the people of the past and their motivations and have learned something about the past – and the present day – in the process. But no matter how powerful the medium, it is worth reminding ourselves that what students experience in this kind of work is *drama* and should be considered as such. Our primary concern therefore has been to provide engaging drama experiences which will enable students to 'handle' the content more authentically, and that the quality of student engagement is key, whatever the desired learning. We hope that teachers from other disciplines will agree, and encourage them to bring their own perspectives, aims and assessment, where appropriate, to the work; we feel that this would be a beneficial process to all involved.

Using the teaching units

The teaching units in this book, although diverse in content, all adhere to a similar format.

We have attempted to structure the units themselves in layers of increasing sophistication and complexity. Starting from relatively simple beginnings, each stage adds another dimension to the potential learning opportunities available. In many of the units the work unfolds in such a way that a number of particular investigations can take place – across a range of curriculum areas, and suitable for learners of varying experience and ability. We encourage teachers to select from the wealth of material available to suit their own needs – and those of the students they teach.

Throughout the units, **contextual information** (stimulus material, resource sheets, script excerpts, etc.) necessary to the units appears in shaded text boxes.

Also folded into the units are **cross-curricular connections** and **additional tasks** – which might make good cover-lesson or homework tasks – and details on **drama strategies and techniques**.

Resources suitable for student handouts are available on the book website as pdf downloads. The website is: www.routledge.com/9780415572064

Foundlings

Foundling: a child who has been abandoned and whose parents are unknown.

Thematic content in this unit:	Curriculum connections:
Folk tales and legends	Literacy, Literature, History
Museums and curation	History, Social Studies, Leisure and Tourism
The history of The Foundling Hospital (C18)	Social History, Citizenship
Moral and emotional aspects of parenting and abandonment	PSHE, Citizenship, SEAL, Geography
An introduction to the work of Bertolt Brecht	Drama

Dramatic techniques and keywords in this unit:

The use of visual stimulus/pretext	Dramatic reconstruction	Depiction
Ritual	Mantle of the expert	Montage
Tableau and tableaux vivants	Staging a text	Commemoration
Teacher in role	Choral work	Physicalization
Symbol	Tension	Atmosphere

In this unit, students will explore the theme of *foundlings*. As stated in the introduction, and in common with other units, the drama is structured in layers of increasing sophistication and complexity. Starting from relatively simple beginnings, each layer adds another dimension to the potential learning opportunities available. The work unfolds in such a way that a number of particular investigations can take place – across a wide range of curriculum areas and suitable for learners of varying experience and ability – but from a common 'holding form': a drama structure that brings coherence to the unit as a whole.

In this case the work is constructed around the idea that students work in role as curators of a foundling 'museum', charged with researching, selecting, creating and presenting various 'exhibits' worthy to be brought before the public. The 'exhibits' are based upon examples of foundling children which the students will investigate as the work progresses. All of these foundling children are brought to life through drama and are fictional; some are based on factual accounts, whilst others take us into the realms of literature and myth. Teachers can, of course, select the particular elements of the work appropriate to the learners in their care. They can also select in which order to play out the various sections of the unit, although the first sections of the unit take a little time to establish the context and holding form of the work.

Where this unit connects

This unit provides opportunities for learning in a number of curriculum areas. In developing a fictional 'foundling museum' students will explore aspects of eighteenth century history, as well as considering the moral and social issues surrounding the giving-up of children in a historical and contemporary context which clearly connects with **PSHE**, **Geography** and **RE** curricula. They will also develop work based around folk tales, and will be introduced to a key twentieth-century European play: opportunities that will link with English – literacy, language and literature. Throughout the unit students will be able to develop skills in a range of oral techniques as they plan and present their drama, working collaboratively in a variety of group sizes and combinations.

Working in drama: by the end of this unit students will have:

- Developed animated *tableaux vivants* to physicalize a 'story plaque' based on a legend.

- Used ritual elements and expressive movement to create atmosphere, tension and mood.

- Interacted with a teacher in role to advise and make decisions which develop the drama, and consider the implications of the developing work.

- Used drama to speculate on events from the past.

- Devised and performed enacted reconstructions and considered how drama can deal with heightened emotion.

- Worked in role as museum curators creating fictionalized but realistic depictions of real events.

- Devised and enacted drama based on a classic play script, before exploring the text itself through choral speaking and physical drama.

Section one

Figure 1.1 Babes in the Wood

These pretty babes with hand in hand went wandering up and down – from the illustrated version by Francis Caldecott, 1879

> He took the children by the hand,
> While teares stood in their eye,
> And bade them come and go with him,
> And look they did not crye:
>
> And two long miles he ledd them on,
> While they for food complaine:
> "Stay here," quoth he, "I'll bring ye bread,
> When I come back againe."
> These prettye babes, with hand in hand,
> Went wandering up and downe;
> But never more they sawe the man
> Approaching from the town.
>
> Their prettye lippes with blackberries
> Were all besmear'd and dyed;
> And when they sawe the darksome night,
> They sat them downe and cryed.
> Thus wandered these two prettye babes,
> Till death did end their grief;
> In one another's armes they dyed,
> As babes wanting relief.
> No burial these prettye babes
> Of any man receives,
> Till Robin-redbreast painfully
> Did cover them with leaves.

The tale *Babes in the Wood* is familiar to many of us as a pantomime – usually with a happy ending when Robin Hood and his Merry Men miraculously rescue the children, abandoned by the brigands hired by their dying parents! In fact, *Babes in the Wood* is a traditional tale, and like many such tales is considerably darker than the sanitized versions which may be familiar to our students. In the folklore of the county of Norfolk, in Eastern England, *Babes in the Wood* is given a convincing local setting in Wayland (or 'Wailing') Wood, near the village of Watton:

> *Two children are due to inherit their father's estate when they come of age. Their parents die and they are entrusted to their uncle. In the terms of the will, if the children die before they come of age then the estate passes to the uncle. The uncle decides to get rid of them and pays two men to take the children into Wayland Wood ('Wailing Wood') and kill them. However, the children's innocence touches one of the brigands, and the two men fight. The more sympathetic of the two kills the other and instead of killing the children they are abandoned in the wood. They never find their way out. In the story the woodland birds cover over their dead bodies with ivy.*
>
> *According to the legend there used to be a huge oak in Wayland Wood, which was said to be the place where they died. Not far from the wood is Griston Hall, said to have been the uncle's house. Inside the hall there used to be a carved plaque depicting the story. It was placed there by a family member in order to remind later relatives of the family's grisly past.*

There are many printed versions of the tale, notably Francis Caldecott's beautiful illustrated version, published in England in the 1870s.[1] In our teaching of this unit we have used projected images from the Caldecott picture book, as well as music – such as the folk song sung by the Copper family of Rottingdean in Sussex – to create atmosphere and tension.

Stage one – exploring the story

In this section, the story of *Babes in the Wood* is approached obliquely through a framing device which projects forward in time from the actual abandonment in the wood, and keys into the part of the legend relating to the evil uncle's house, Griston Hall.

If the students are not familiar with the story either tell it to them, or have them research the various versions available. We have found it useful to create a slide show of the evocative Caldecott illustrations referred to above.

Tell the students of the legend of Griston Hall – and ask them to imagine that in the large, wood-panelled dining room of the hall is the plaque depicting the story, carved to remind later descendants of the uncle's ill doings. The plaque was carved out of wood from the large oak tree underneath which the children died.

Ask the students to consider what the plaque might show – bearing in mind that it was constructed to serve as a warning or reminder. It may be useful at this point to provide examples of other plaques or friezes – or even paintings – which depict a sequence of events in order to act as a commemoration or as remembrance.

- Does the plaque simply depict episodes from the story?

- Are the images realistic or stylized – perhaps grotesque?

Working in groups of two or three, ask the students to create sections of the plaque as *tableaux* or *still images*.

Present the tableaux as a sequence – chronologically if that is appropriate – and interrogate the images in order to clarify meanings and give the students an opportunity to reflect on the overall effect of their work.

---

*Group-devised **tableaux** or **still images** are often used in drama teaching, particularly in the early stages of the students' explorations, to clarify a particular moment in a drama, define a theme or explore an idea, potentially with economy, control and precision. However, tableaux are sometimes over-used and, like all techniques, have their limitations:

- Tableaux, like photographs, are essentially *compositions:* they are, in effect, *mini stage pictures*, to be de-coded or 'read' by an 'audience'. Aesthetic and formal considerations (such as the students' use of 'levels' to emphasize status, or their use of stylized gesture to signal the isolation of a character) can give the work added significance. Young or inexperienced students may need to be alerted to the potential for tableaux to make complex or abstract ideas concrete, as well as their use in crystallizing a moment in a 'realistic' improvisation or play text.

- Group-devised tableaux presented to the rest of the group can also present logistical problems: devising and presenting tends to have its own dynamic in the classroom with groups keen to present their work; the average group size of 30 often produces 10 working groups. If all groups present (and then evaluate) their work in the traditional way, this can give undue emphasis to relatively minor tasks. In our experience, 'spotlighting' particular groups as exemplars, or presenting the tableaux in sequence without interruption followed by summary reflection on the work, can alleviate the problem.

- Related to this is the fact that tableaux, particularly presented by inexperienced students, will often be unclear or ambiguous. At its worst this can result in the class attempting to guess what and who is being represented. More experienced students will become adept at using tableaux to signal *sub-text* – what is happening 'beneath the surface' of a relationship or situation, but at first many groups find this challenging. For these reasons it is useful to 'interrogate' the depictions in order to clarify and deepen the work:

  o groups can be asked to give their tableaux titles, captions or 'labels' which are spoken by members of the group;

  o characters in the tableau can be questioned by the teacher – or the class. Be sure that students understand that they must respond *as the character*, not as themselves;

  o characters, likewise, can be asked to speak their thoughts – or other members of the group can be asked to speak their thoughts for them (*thought-tracking*).

In tableaux tasks where all the working groups have been asked to represent different versions of the same incident or moment, it can be useful to ask all of the pupils representing a given character (for example the 'mother of the bride' in a wedding scenario) to 'step out' of their group tableau, and present their part of the tableau in the centre of the room in isolation from its original context. In this way it is possible for a class to compare the various representations of a particular character, and to interpret the representations in terms of their similar or contrasting physicality.

It can also be useful to ask groups to 'bring their tableau to life' for a short period (perhaps 15–20 seconds). This immediately clarifies the context of an image, and can emphasize the importance of 'freezing' a tableau at a crucial moment in a situation – often the moment *before* a crisis or climax.

Tableaux can also be used to structure and construct movement sequences in various ways, perhaps by 'morphing' one image into another, or by 'animating' the tableaux using stylized repetitive movement – as in a 'flick-book' animation. By using minimal but repeated movement in this manner simple tableaux can be become sophisticated expressive tools. (For a detailed example of this way of working see Lewis and Rainer (2005), pp. 115–16.)

Ask the students to imagine that many years later, Griston Hall is to be sold and that the plaque is still intact. Reforming their original tableaux, ask the students to consider what the plaque might have witnessed over several hundred years – family events, births, funerals or marriages; perhaps scandals, wars or famines. Ask each student in turn to speak 'as if' they were the plaque. Try to maintain a ritual element: *I have witnessed . . .*

Remind the students that the hall is due to be sold, and for the first time will be owned by someone outside the family. It is rumoured that they may refurbish the hall and destroy the dusty, old-fashioned plaque.

What might the plaque think about that? If it could speak, what would it say?

Explain that in the sequence that follows the plaque is able to come to life, section by section, but only for a short time – say 15 seconds. During that time the plaque is able to speak and move, and will be able to plead to be retained in the hall and not destroyed.

Ask the students to reform their tableaux once more. Adopt the role of the buyer of the hall preparing plans for the new dining room.

Teaching in role is a flexible and sophisticated means of teaching that is probably worthy of a book to itself!

However, in our experience when working in role with a class, the key things to remember are:

- Consider carefully the *function* of the TiR sequence within the unit of work as a whole. This could range from simple information-giving (exposition), to helping to build belief in the context of a drama, to enabling students to gain a change in perspective, introducing a dilemma or problem, or heightening the students' emotional and intellectual engagement in the work.

- Consider carefully the *status* of the role being portrayed. High status roles will feel comfortable to inexperienced teachers but are less likely to result in classes becoming fully engaged and contributing their own ideas; low status roles have the potential to boost students' confidence and encourage creative responses, but are perhaps more risky for teachers concerned about their own authority and power in the classroom.

- Be sure that the students understand their own role and perspective within an in-role encounter. It is always useful to stop, and check for understanding. (*In the drama, who was I* (the teacher) *portraying? Did you like that person? Did you trust them? Who were you in the drama? When and where was it set?* etc.)

- Remember that teaching in role is essentially *experiential*; we are attempting to lead our students through a rich, but improvised, fictional encounter which will ultimately influence their understanding of the social world. It is inappropriate when working in this way to focus on 'performance skills' (i.e., to criticize students who are responding to you in role because of their diction or gesture – or because they 'turned their back to the audience'!). This has implications for the style of 'acting' that is appropriate for working in role: it is a minimal style, economical in its use of 'signs' – unlike some forms of 'stage acting'. However, when working in role you should attempt to create a physical presence and also to build tension, atmosphere and mood through the role. Teaching in role is not therefore simply 'mouthing someone else's words'. In finding an appropriate style, don't forget that whilst working in role you are modelling for the class the 'acting' style that you desire them to adopt. If you self-consciously perform for the class it is likely that they will reciprocate, with the result that the work may lack integrity and depth.[2]

As you approach each section of the 'plaque' as the 'new owner' it will come to life. Allow students time in their groups to prepare their work.

Will the plaque (for instance):

- Give reasons why it is important that it should be retained in the hall?
- Attempt to scare the owner into relinquishing the sale?

Remind the group that as the plaque depicts characters from the original tale, that these can also 'come to life' – with rich dramatic potential, perhaps?

Once prepared, enact the sequence, perhaps using lighting and sound to enhance mood and create tension.

In terms of plenary reflection the following questions may focus the groups' responses:

- What is it that is interesting about the story of *Babes in the Wood?* Why is it perhaps unlike other traditional stories?
- Why do some objects seem to retain their 'power' even amongst people who are not superstitious? For instance, a fountain pen used by a writer thought to be a genius, or a pair of gloves worn by a mass-murderer, would affect most people in some way. What does the plaque in the story come to symbolize?

Stage two – the abandoned child

To begin this section the teacher takes on the role of a forester who has found an abandoned baby (represented by a bundle) whilst working in a remote corner of the woods. The person is taken aback by finding the seemingly abandoned child, is ignorant of the needs of babies – and devoid of parenting skills!

The aim here is to use the fictional role to engage the students, and arouse their interest in the developing context of the drama. We have found that whilst in role at this point, deliberately remaining a somewhat ambiguous figure – not answering students' questions directly, and certainly not providing definitive or conclusive solutions to problems or issues raised – can create an air of intrigue which motivates students to want to find out more.

Whilst playing through this section we aim to:

1 Create a sense of 'place'; a 'stage set' – perhaps with the 'baby' in a wicker basket – and as mentioned above, use projected images and music to enhance the mood of mystery.

2 Introduce the role of the Forester gradually, letting the context emerge – *'I found this baby. I don't know how to take care of it ... do you?'*

3 Develop the work by introducing a task orientation to the drama:
 Once students have begun to engage with the situation we then introduce a cloth bag of objects seemingly acquired by the Forester in the woods. This will include a range of items – feeding bottle, nappy, etc., which may assist the care of the baby, but will also include things that would clearly be of limited or no use; perhaps a saw or a hammer. *I brought some stuff that might be useful ... are these any use?*

4   Create tension in the situation:

The Forester is, of course, completely ignorant of childcare:

*How **do** you take care of a baby?*

The idea here is to empower the students to begin to take some control of the situation – and perhaps to begin to feel exasperated by the stupidity of the adult character, so that they will *want* to take over.

Depending on the class, and the time available, this section could be developed into a range of cross-curricular tasks. For instance students might move beyond simply giving advice to the forester, and could begin to construct a 'manual' or presentation on 'how to care for babies'.

History/personal, social and health education

This exercise will explore the changing nature of being a parent over the last century and ask students to consider the role of families within the twenty-first century. Look at the following list of trends from family life in Britain at the beginning of the twentieth.

In pairs, discuss your experiences of what it is like to be a member of a family now. Are there any significant differences from 100 years ago? Ask your teacher for help if you are unsure.

Twentieth century:

- Women could not vote and had few legal rights.

- Men were the chief wage earners and providers.

- Married women stayed at home and looked after the children.

- Families with lots of children were very common.

- *Spare the rod and spoil the child* along with *children should be seen and not heard* were common phrases.

- Crowded cities and poor quality housing were a feature of everyday life for many.

- Divorce was seen as a disgrace and divorced women had no rights to the family home or any financial support.

Task: for each comment, write down what you think is the twenty-first century experience of family life. Rehearse this as a short presentation to the rest of the group. Are there any other differences you might be able to find by researching on the Internet or going to the library?

Alternatively, create a table in a Microsoft Word document or, using images found from the Internet, compose a poster for display in the classroom.

---

5   Deepen students' thinking:

At this point the TIR needs to introduce questions that might deepen the students' response to the drama and will shift their thinking into a consideration of the affective and moral power of the situation:

Foundlings

Who do you think its mother is? Why has she left it?

These important considerations will be developed further in what follows.

6 Give the students power to make decisions within the fiction:

What should we do with the baby? Will you help me find someone to look after it?

I know two people who would like to look after it. Could you speak to them and choose which one would make the best parent?

This last episode could give students opportunities to consider issues relating to parenting as they interview two possible 'carers' for the child (both, of course, portrayed by the teacher in role), and decide which would be most suitable.

Personal, social and health education

Parenthood – how parents' lives change after the birth of a baby.

It is true to say that very young babies are hard work to look after! Ask students to form groups of four. Remind them that they will not remember the times when they themselves were extremely young babies, but they may have heard stories told about their early days and months by other members of the family. Alternatively they might be able to remember younger siblings and the exploits and adventures they got up to during those first few months and years. Ask the group to share some of those stories with each other.

Task: on paper, ask the students to make two columns. Title one 'Before Baby' and the other 'After Baby . . .' Now think of the changes faced by parents of a newborn and begin to fill in the list.

For instance:

- *Before Baby* . . . we could sleep all night.

- *After Baby* . . . we have to get up lots of times in the middle of the night.

- *Before Baby* . . . we didn't know what a nappy was.

- *After Baby* . . . we certainly do now.

Encourage students to not just think of 'negatives': think of the positive parts of being a new mum or dad too – there really are lots and they should outweigh the negatives!

As an extension task students could compose a short poem using some of their ideas.

The teacher now comes out of role – placing the baby back down as part of the 'set' – and asks a key question to aid students' reflection and deepen thinking on the previous work:

Why would someone abandon their baby?

Try to categorize students' speculative responses:

- The child's mother was unmarried – perhaps the child was abandoned to hide her shame – or out of a desire to conceal? Perhaps she was *forced* to abandon the child?

- To save the child from harm? For instance, the child might be the heir to a great fortune, or even a disputed throne?

- Poverty? Perhaps the family could not afford to feed the child?

- War/revolution? Perhaps the child (like Michael in Brecht's *Caucasian Chalk Circle*) was caught up in the chaos caused by people being displaced or running away?

- A curse or superstition? Perhaps the family or community believe that the child will cause harm?

Stage three – the Foundling Hospital

> *If Fortune should her favours give*
> *That I in Better plight may Live*
> *I'd try to have my boy again*
> *And Train him up the best of Men*
>
> (Written for a child named Joseph, born in 1759 and left at 14 days old.)

In this section the theme of *foundlings* becomes more firmly established as students are introduced to the Foundling Hospital, founded by the philanthropist Thomas Coram in 1739.

This section of the work will need to be handled with some sensitivity, dealing as it does, with the abandonment of infants.

> *In eighteenth-century England, abandoning babies was commonplace: Thomas Coram himself was outraged at seeing dead babies abandoned on dung-heaps in London.*
>
> *Between 1756 and 1760 – the era of 'basket babies' or 'general reception' – the hospital was forced to accept all foundlings under two months of age. During this period 14,934 children were received; 10,204 died.*
>
> *Children received were immediately given new names, and the children were never told of the birth tokens left with them by anguished parents.*
>
> *Some people made money by agreeing to transport unwanted children to the Foundling Hospital from further afield. Many of the children died – or in some cases were killed before they arrived. One story tells of a man transporting eight children from some distance away. Only one baby survived the journey, and that was because its mother walked behind the wagon for the entire journey.*

Using the bundle, which previously represented the child found in the woods, explain to the students that we are now going to turn our attention to another child from a different time and place – a long time ago:

Foundlings

*The person who left **this** baby took it to a hospital. In the hospital there was a hole in the wall. The mother put her baby in, and rang the bell, and someone came to get the baby. And that was the last time she saw the baby.*

Working in twos, ask the students to decide the circumstances of the mother giving up her baby. Ask them to give the child a name.

At this stage the context of the work for the students is still rather vague – for instance, the precise period in which the drama is set, and its location, is unstated. As the work unfolds the context will become clearer for the students. Reassure them to this effect if necessary.

Now working in role as (a) the mother of the child and (b) another significant adult (father of the child, parent, or other relative of the mother, perhaps), ask the students to enact the 30 seconds of action leading to the child being left at the hospital. Ask for volunteers, and share the work.

As students in turn enact the last moments before the child is given up, ask the rest of the class to watch carefully and note anything that they think is significant. If appropriate, these fragments of drama can be replayed, and significant moments can be frozen, and/or characters can be questioned in role or 'thought-tracked'. Ask the students to reflect upon their feelings at this stage.

This hospital really existed – it was built in London 270 years ago. Hundreds of children were left at the hospital in the way we have seen – the baby was placed in a basket and a bell was rung ... Each child left was between 2 months and 1 year old; each was left with a 'token', which might be a keepsake for the child and would enable the mother to reclaim her child at a later date.

In the same pairs, ask the students to draw on cards a sketch of the birth token left with the child by its mother:

A small and perhaps insignificant object becoming something precious beyond monetary value ...

Once this task is complete ask the students to mount their 'birth tokens' in the 'foundling museum' – a well-lit section of classroom wall is ideal.

The teacher now adopts the role of the Director of the museum:

Now I know that you have been researching some foundling children for our museum. What have you found out ...?

Ask students – in their pairs – to speak – as 'historians' – about the child that they have 'researched'. This switch in role – from the parent of the fictional foundling, to someone in the present day researching the same child – is a key moment as it enables the students to switch perspective on the work, and enables them – almost literally – to see the episode through 'different eyes'.

Besides aiding students' understanding, this switch in role perspective can also take some of the emotional 'heat' out of the previous section of the drama.

What did you find out about the children you were researching? What does the birth token left with the foundling tell us about the circumstances that forced the mother to give up her child?

Ask the students to add other information to their 'birth tokens' in the form of annotations, exhibit cards or labels, and place them in the foundling museum.

Once the 'museum' is complete, ask the students to adopt the role of visitors to the museum, and allow some time for them to examine each 'exhibit'.

Now, if we were the curators of this museum, and space was limited, we would be forced with a difficult choice: which exhibits should we place on permanent exhibition, and why?

Encourage students to return to the exhibits, and select those they feel should stay, stressing that they should be able to justify their choices.

Give realistic time for discussion. It is not important to come to a conclusion, but the teacher should be ready to ask questions to deepen the students' thinking about the problem they face.

As a conclusion to this section, out of role, the students may find it interesting to know that there is a real museum in London commemorating foundlings, and that within it there is a large gallery of birth tokens left with children over many years.[3]

If we are to commemorate these children, what would we want to add to our museum?

Perhaps we need other examples of different kinds of 'foundlings' to show visitors to our 'foundling museum'?

Figure 1.2 Birth tokens on display at the Foundling Museum, London

Foundlings

Stage four – the temptation to do good

We include this section as an example of how the 'holding form' of the 'foundling museum', once established, can be used to teach a wide range of particular topics from across the curriculum. In this example we develop the idea of 'researching other kinds of foundlings' to lead students into an initial exploration of a long and complex play, Bertolt Brecht's *The Caucasian Chalk Circle*.

Modern-day foundlings

It is estimated that around 60 babies a year are abandoned in the United Kingdom. These modern-day foundlings are often placed in areas where they will be discovered quickly such as on doorsteps or in telephone boxes, public toilets, hospitals or airports.

Once discovered, the babies are medically assessed and looked after while the police attempt to find the mother. If either parent cannot be traced, then the child is taken into care until a full-time foster family can be found.

There may be many reasons why a mother might act in such a way but as most of the parents are never traced, the foundlings are left with lots of questions and very few answers. For these children, all the things that most of us take for granted such as a name, age and family history are missing.

Task: use the Internet and the library to research into some of the real-life stories and accounts of being a modern-day foundling. As a starting point, find out about Steve Hydes who became known as the 'Gatwick Baby' after he was discovered on the floor of the ladies', toilet in the airport in 1986.

Using one of the stories that you have investigated, prepare a two minute television news item reporting on the plight of abandoned children. You could experiment with the narrative of the report by including flashback where we see the reasons why a child was left and flash-forward; the child as an adult reflecting upon their life as a foundling.

In this play, set in the Soviet Union after the Second World War, Brecht presents a 'play-within-a-play' – a parable about the abandonment of a baby during a civil war – in order to help two groups of Russian collective farmers decide how to allocate some disputed farming land. In the parable, a servant girl named Grusha is confronted with a difficult choice: should she take, and care for, the baby boy abandoned by his mother in her hurry to flee the civil war?

The beginning of this sequence uses the same starting point as the previous work: a baby – in this case draped in rich velvet – in a basket.

This baby's mother was very rich. She left her baby because she had to flee a civil war, a revolution. She left it behind. It was the heir to a great fortune . . .

A servant found the baby. She didn't know whether to pick it up and care for it or not. Why do you think she might have hesitated?

Ask for a volunteer to represent Grusha the kitchen maid, and enact the moment – she sits with the child and isn't sure what to do.

Ask the class to speak:

a) ... the girl's thoughts; what was her inner voice telling her?

b) ... as if the baby could speak?

c) ... the advice her fellow servants would give?

d) ... as the child's mother.

Grusha finally makes the decision to take the baby.

In groups of five ask the students to enact their own version of the moment that Grusha finally decides to pick up the child and take it with her: one of them should represent Grusha, and the others portray the various 'voices' outlined in the previous exercise.

Leave some working time and then present the work. Ask them to consider their dramas as possible *living exhibits* in the museum:

This will form another exhibit in the foundling museum. Its title will be:

TERRIBLE IS THE TEMPTATION TO DO GOOD.

Why might this be a good title for this exhibit?

What else could we add to our exhibit?

The action of the students' drama so far closely mirrors Act 1 Scene 2 of Brecht's play. In the final section we introduce students to some of the text of the play. The following text is narrated, or sung, by 'The Singer' – the ballad singer hired by the collective farms to help resolve the dispute. Throughout the parable that he and the other actors enact, The Singer constantly interrupts the action to comment upon it, and to speak the thoughts of the characters:

Foundlings

As she was standing between courtyard and gate, she heard
Or thought she heard, a low voice. The child
Called to her, not whining but calling quite sensibly:
At least so it seemed to her: 'Woman', it said, 'Help me'.

Don't you know, woman, that she who does not listen to
a cry for help
But passes by shutting her ears, will never hear
The gentle call of a lover
Nor the blackbird at dawn, nor the happy
Sigh of the exhausted grape-picker at the sound of the Angelus.

Hearing this
She went back to the child
Just for one more look, just to sit with it
For a moment or two till someone should come
Its mother perhaps, or someone else
Just for a moment before she left, for now the danger was too great,
The city full of flame and grief.

Terrible is the temptation to do good!

For a long time she sat with the child.
Evening came, night came, dawn came.
Too long she sat, too long she watched
The soft breathing, the little fists
Till towards morning the temptation grew too strong.
She rose, she leaned over, she sighed, she lifted the child
She carried it off.
Like booty she took it for herself
Like a thief she sneaked away.

Project the text onto a large screen. We have sub-divided the text into five sections so that the same groups might work on the next task. Teachers can, of course, make different decisions about the way that the text is divided up to suit their own purposes. In this case we have differentiated the task by simply altering the length of the sections.

Once groups are formed, allocate a section of text to each group.

Ask students to base their work upon the previous task: the only action in the scene is that which they have already explored: Grusha sits all night with the child, and finally takes it. They are to add the text to the sequence they have already constructed.

Encourage them to experiment with ways of breaking up their section of text amongst the members of the group. Some of it could be spoken chorally; repeated or echoed sections might also be effective. Perhaps their original version could be juxtaposed with the Brecht to create a composite version or montage?

Choral speaking

Choral speaking of a text can be a powerful expressive form, particularly when combined with movement or 'physical theatre'. A range of techniques can be explored, including:

- Chanting in unison.

- Echoing effects.

- Experimenting with pitch, dynamics and timbre.

- Breaking the text down in various ways, and 'sharing' it amongst the group: paragraphs; verses; lines; words; syllables.

Bear it in mind that the more the text is broken down in this way, the more 'abstract' the work is likely to become, with textual meaning giving way to 'musical' effect. Remember, also, that whilst detailed work of this kind can be theatrically very effective, it can also be very time consuming for students to devise and to 'choreograph'.

As a preliminary exercise for less experienced students, encourage the class to experiment with techniques to create specific effects – comic, or sinister, robotic, or highly atmospheric renderings of small sections of a simple text – perhaps a nursery rhyme – before moving on to the main task.

Finally, ask the groups to present their work to each other. Ask other group members to view the dramatic sequences as living exhibits in the foundling museum.

In the plenary discussion encourage the students to reflect upon whether the foundling frame has helped motivate them to want to study more of the play!

The frame now established – of the foundling museum – is extremely flexible and can be used to explore a wide range of thematic and cross-curricular topics. Below we list some suggestions:

Foundlings

Oedipus – A herdsman is ordered to kill him – abandoned in the hills and left to die, he later grows up to unwittingly marry his mother. **(History, English, Drama)**

Snow White – A servant is given orders to kill her, but again abandons her. **(English)**

The Winter's Tale – Perdita turns out to be a princess rather than a shepherdess, and is therefore able to marry her prince. **(English, Drama)**

Superman – Sent to earth from an advanced but dying planet. Found by Kansas farmers and raised as their own. Later discovers his alien origin and uses his powers for good. **(Science, Art, English, Media, Geography)**

Orphans and foundlings in the work of *Charles Dickens* – in particular *Oliver Twist*, who finds his birth family with a locket left by his mother. **(English, History)**

Fielding's *Tom Jones*. **(English, History)**

The story of *Moses*. **(RE)**

Contemporary parallels to the Foundling Hospital – *'foundling wheels'*, *'stork's cradles'* and *'baby hatches'*. **(PSHE, H&SC, Geography)**

Coram Boy by Jamila Gavin – a children's novel based around this theme – adapted as a National Theatre 'Connections' stage play. **(English, Drama, History)**

The resources for this Unit are available for download at www.routledge.com/9780415572064

Van Diemen's Land

Thematic content in this unit:	Curriculum connections:
How meaning is created in drama	Drama, English, Media Studies
Folk songs and ballads	History, English, Music
The colonization and development of Australia	Geography, History
The British Empire	Geography, History
Crime and punishment	History, Citizenship
Justice and fairness	Citizenship
Transportation and penal colonies	History
Aboriginal art, customs and legends	Art and Design, RE, English
Information posters	Art and Design, Media Studies

Dramatic techniques and keywords in this unit:

Sign	Symbol
Denotation	Connotation
Dramatic metaphor	Using drama to speculate in history
Empathy	

This unit invites students to speculate about specific historical events, using drama as an investigative tool, and provides opportunities for students to create performances based on their exploratory work. It employs a variety of stimulus materials – including contemporary ballads and posters relating specifically to the penal colony of Van Diemen's Land, which provide interesting insights into the lives of people of the time.

Van Diemen's Land

   The drama in this unit takes place in a specific time and place – the penal colony of Van Diemen's Land (later Tasmania) in the early nineteenth century. It investigates aspects of the history of the colony and allows students to explore the feelings and motivations of people in the past. In using drama in this manner we are aware of potential pitfalls. Students working within historical contexts should always be reminded that what they are experiencing is fiction, not history; as we suggest in the introduction to this book, good drama is often poor history, and vice-versa. In the suggested activities we hope to exploit something of drama's potential to alter perspective by providing an opportunity to explore the situation from three different viewpoints, as students adopt the roles of British administrators, convicts and indigenous Australians. In so doing we are hoping to facilitate empathetic responses from students; asking them to identify to some degree with the characters they portray. Empathy, as we also discuss in the introduction, is itself a problematic concept. Whilst conscious of the controversies surrounding the use of that term in history teaching in recent years, we hope that amongst drama teachers the idea that students might seek to sense something of what the world must be like from the perspective of another is less problematic: it is surely the basis of all acting. Whilst recognizing that there are limits on the extent to which students can truly empathize with people in particular historical contexts, in this unit we hope that in creating their fictions, students might glean some insight into the motivations and dilemmas of real people who lived in the past, might question their assumptions and world view, and, in so doing, might begin to see the world of the present from a different angle.

> *Empathizing . . . It's about being able to imagine what someone else is thinking or feeling, and having an emotional response to the other person's feelings.*
> Dr Simon Baron-Cohen

The tasks also invite students to explore the use of metaphors in drama, starting with simple definitional exercises, and developing into more extended dramatic metaphors.[1]

Where this unit connects

This unit is firmly based in an investigation of historical events that occurred in the late eighteenth and early nineteenth centuries, in a land far distant, geographically and culturally, from our own. Using historical primary source material (see also p. 62), it uses drama to help students gain insight into the events of the period, and also to begin to trace connections with our own epoch. It asks students to consider issues of crime, punishment and justice, poses the problem of communication with people who do not share a language or a culture, and uses a folk ballad of the time as a vehicle for creative dramatizations of the past.

> **Working in drama: by the end of this unit students will have:**
>
> - Explored the use of signs, symbols and metaphors in drama.
>
> - Used a variety of dramatic techniques to speculate about and re-enact past events.
>
> - Worked in role with a teacher to give life to an imagined context.

Section one

In the early nineteenth century, people could be transported to penal colonies abroad for relatively minor crimes. As an introduction to the unit, students will have the opportunity to make a drama structured around a transportation ballad of the time, a folk song known as *Van Diemen's Land*.

Stage one

Introduce yourself to the class – in role – as one of the characters from the transportation ballad, *Van Diemen's Land*, referenced above.

Let me tell you a little of my story. I'm Tom Brown from Nottingham. I was caught stealing when I was fifteen and now they intend to transport me to Van Diemen's Land to serve a term of seven years. It can't be right: me and my family were hungry ...

Allow the class to *hot-seat* Tom to establish some of the detail. Try to engage the class' interest in what might lie in store for Tom: it may be effective to 'play' Tom as young and ignorant of his fate:

- *What do you think it'll be like out there?*

- *How long will it take my ship to get there?*

- *I hear the place is full of strange creatures – can it be true?*

Explain that they will be using drama – and a 'pop song' of the time, to find out a little more about people like Tom.

Van Diemen's Land

Come all you gallant poachers that ramble free from care
That walk out of a moonlight night with your dog your gun and snare
Where the lofty hare and pheasant you have at your command
Not thinking that your last career is on Van Diemen's Land

There was poor Tom Brown from Nottingham Jack Williams and poor Joe
Were three as daring poachers as the country well does know
At night they were trepanned by the keeper's hideous hand
And for fourteen years transported were unto Van Diemen's Land
Oh when we sailed from England we landed at the bay
We had rotten straw for bedding we dared not to say nay
Our cots were fenced with fire we slumber when we can
To drive away the wolves and tigers upon Van Diemen's Land

Oh when that we were landed upon that fatal shore
The planters they came flocking round full twenty score or more
They ranked us up like horses and sold us out of hand
They yoked us up to the plough my boys to plough Van Diemen's Land

There was one girl from England Susan Summers was her name
For fourteen years transported was we all well knew the same
Our planter bought her freedom and he married her out of hand
Good usage then she gave to us upon Van Diemen's Land

Often when I am slumbering I have a pleasant dream
With my sweet girl I am sitting down by some purling stream
Through England I am roaming with her at my command
Then waken broken hearted upon Van Diemen's Land

God bless our wives and families likewise that happy shore
That isle of sweet contentment which we shall see no more
As for our wretched females see them we seldom can
There are twenty to one woman upon Van Diemen's Land

Come all you gallant poachers give ear unto my song
It is a bit of good advice although it is not long
Lay by your dog and snare to you I do speak plain
If you knew the hardship we endure you ne'er would poach again

Van Diemen's Land

Figure 2.1 Music score

Stage two

Form groups of five; give each group a copy of the transportation ballad *Van Diemen's Land.* Allow the groups time to read the text through.

The ballad provides some clues to start the groups' dramatizations, for instance:

- What is the main character (the singer) called? What about other characters?
- What information is given about their life before transportation?
- What details are given of their crimes?

Using the text of the ballad as a starting point, ask the students to create a sequence of three still images:

- What life was like for the person before the crime was committed.
- The crime itself.
- Their discovery or arrest.

Once the tableaux have been presented, ask the group to use them as a basis for developing three short (one minute) scenes.

How effectively have these short scenes conveyed something of the background to the stories of those transported like Tom?

Folk songs and ballads

Folk songs are songs that are rooted in the popular culture and traditions of a particular country or area, or songs that are composed in that style. *Traditional* songs are so called because who composed them is not known. Very often – like stories – they have been passed from person to person and over the years may exist in many different variants in different parts of the world.

Task: research any folk songs from the area in which you live. There may be rural songs, relating to farming and country pursuits, songs that celebrate particular industries such as mining or fishing, songs relating to immigration, loss and parting, or simple love songs.

It may be easier to collect the words than the melodies; if so, compose your own tune and chordal accompaniment to fit the words of the songs that you found.

Stage three

Ask the groups to return to the ballad text. Explain to the group that they will now use the ballad as the basis for a piece of drama that will symbolize the nine-month ship journey to Van Diemen's Land.

Ask each group to select one or more verses from the ballad to use as a basis for a further scene: an event that took place in the past, on board ship, or a scene that might be a projection into the future. The ballad itself can act as a structure for the drama: a group member might recite or sing it as the scenes are enacted, or the group itself could use choral techniques to speak the verses as part of the dramatic action.

Present the dramas, once rehearsed, as a sequence, which tells the story of a group of convicts arriving at the penal colony of Van Diemen's Land. Ask the class to speculate as to what might have happened to the convicts. Ask them to research any real life stories they can find (many are available via the Internet). The second part of the drama asks them to take on the role of those who were paid to keep the convicts in order.

There were 220 capital offences in Britain in the early 1800s, many of which did not involve a form of murder: most of them were for stealing and other property crimes.

The system of transportation had some particular advantages to the British Government. It reduced the number of people in prison in Britain, and at the same time provided a source of low cost labour in the colonies.

Prisoners were set to work building all the things that the settlements needed. Any breaches in discipline were dealt with severely by flogging, hard labour and solitary imprisonment.

British officers and administrators, and later 'free' settlers, were awarded large tracts of land which needed a steady supply of labour.

At first convicts outnumbered settlers, and those that had served a reasonable proportion of their sentence were allowed to establish small farms. This tended to be unpopular with the 'free' settlers.

In many places convicts were forced to work as servants for settlers, who in theory were responsible for their upkeep. In practice, however, they were often treated very badly. The government turned a blind eye to this, as it did not have to meet the costs of the convicts' welfare.

Convicts were watched carefully at all times and any who stepped out of line could be sent to a penal settlement, like Norfolk Island or Maquarie Harbour, where treatment was much more severe.

An estimated total of 160,000 convicts were transported to Australia.

Of these, approximately 25,000 were women and girls.

Transportation to Tasmania ceased in 1852, and to Western Australia in 1868.

White men did not 'discover' Australia. By the time Cook arrived in 1770, Aboriginal Australians had lived there for over 30,000 years.

At the time that the first convicts arrived, indigenous Australians lived as 'hunter-gatherers': they kept no stock, ploughed no crops and had no permanent houses.

They lived in nomadic tribal groups, each independent of the other, with no shared language. This made it very difficult for them to co-operate in order to resist as the whites took their land.

Stage four

Explain to the class that they are going to take on the role of a group of people paid by the government to keep order in the colony of Van Diemen's Land. It is the year 1816. It may be worth spending some time establishing a little of the historical context for what is to follow – there are no telephones, TV or computers! To get a message 'home' would take months – even years. Explain that you are going to take on the role of the Governor, who is the man in charge. Ask the class to watch and listen carefully as you work in role, as at this stage there will be a lot of information or contextual 'clues' for them to take in.

Welcome to this celebration supper. God has been kind to us and since we arrived here we have made much progress. We have built our small settlement into a thriving town; our population is growing. You have all made a worthy contribution to the growth of our colony, but we still have much to do. Our main difficulty is in trying to communicate with the Aboriginal people who live nearby. They appear not to trust us. They do not speak our language, and we have no-one who speaks any of their languages. We must communicate our intention: that we intend to treat them fairly – and will treat them as equals within the law . . .

After checking for understanding, find out what clues the class has picked up from this 'exposition'. At this stage, encourage speculative thinking, and don't be in too much of a hurry to define the emerging dramatic context:

- *What do you imagine the colonists feel about serving in Australia?*
- *Who are these people? What might they expect to gain?*
- *What of the Aboriginal people? How might they feel about the colonists?*

Ask the class to consider the colonists problem: how might they communicate? What could they do to help the Aboriginal people understand that they will be treated fairly?

Establishing yourself in role

When working in this exciting way, there is a tendency to move quickly into 'exposition', and then either cut the session short if students are reticent to contribute, or plough on if things seem to be going well. By developing the role more slowly, establishing your character and observing the class carefully you should be able to judge the students' level of engagement. In our experience it is always useful to stop and come out of role in order to:

1) Check for understanding: in the drama,

  - *Who were you?*
  - *Who was I?*
  - *Where were we?*
  - *When?*
  - *What was happening?* (the 'five Ws')

2) Encourage reflection:

  - *What did you think of . . . ?*
  - *Did you trust her?*

  before continuing.

Stage five

One possible course of action for the colonists might be to create posters, using visual symbols to communicate. In groups of four, distribute large sheets of paper and ask the pupils to design a poster that would:

- Communicate with another group of people who have no shared language or culture.
- Demonstrate that they will be treated fairly.
- Show that the law will be applied equally to both colonists and Aboriginal people.

Posters

Obvious links can be made here with students' work in art and design, media studies or PSHE, where they may have had experience in designing posters for a particular audience – perhaps as part of a simulated advertising campaign marketing a product, or as an example of graphic design created for maximum impact on a social issue. (See also Chapter 3, p. 52.)

Once the groups have completed the task, ask them to elect a spokesperson from the group. Explain that the presentation of the various posters will be done in role – at a reconvened 'planning meeting' of the colonists. Again in role as the Governor, the teacher's function in this episode is to manage the meeting, and to probe students to reveal the thinking behind their posters.

Stage six

Once the posters have been presented and discussed, explain to the class that the problem that they have attempted to resolve is based on a real historical example: in 1816 the British administrators of Van Diemen's Land, in an attempt to placate the indigenous Australians, issued posters designed to communicate exactly the same points.

Display the image of the poster of Governor Davy's Proclamation (Figure 2.2).

Ask the students to compare and contrast their own solutions to the 'problem' with the solution found by the colonists. How similar are the posters made by the class? Do they share the use of common signs and symbols?

Stage seven

Ask the class to consider the colonists' motivation for issuing the poster. Do they feel that the offer of justice and fair treatment was genuine? To explore this further, divide the class into groups of four or five. Pin the poster to the wall in a prominent position in the classroom.

Figure 2.2 Governor Davey's Proclamation to the Aborigines 1816
Source: http://images.statelibrary.tas.gov.au

We are going to explore what the people at the time might have felt about this poster.

I want you to imagine that this poster has just been pasted to the walls around the colony. Some of you are going to take on roles of colonists and settlers, and some as Aboriginal people, seeing the poster for the first time. I want each of you to decide on your role. For instance you could be a convict, recently transported from Britain, or a settler who is attempting to gain more land. You could be part of the colonial administration or their families. You could be an indigenous Australian whose people have lived on the land for centuries.

Once the students have selected a role for themselves, ask them to think about their attitude to what is happening. Allow some time for the students to 'rehearse' their roles:

Find a partner: one of you is to remain in role, the other is to ask them questions. Find out what they do, how they live, what their hopes for the future might be.

After an appropriate time, ask the students to swap, so that each has a chance to work in role.

I am going to take on the role of the Lieutenant-Governor, who is the person in charge of the colony. Each of you is to decide on something that you want to say to the Lieutenant-Governor that expresses your feelings about the poster, and perhaps about the situation in general. In addition to this phrase, create an individual tableau which physically symbolizes your response to the poster in a visual image.

'People of Van Diemen's Land! With this I pledge that all will be treated equally within the law: black, white, free man or convict . . .'

Once the groups have made their tableaux, ask them to arrange themselves around the room in relation to the poster. On a given signal ask the students to assume their tableaux. Each student in role is to respond physically and verbally to the Lieutenant-Governor, so that the sequence of students' responses radiate turn by turn around the room with each student taking their 'cue' from the person preceding them in the sequence.

In discussion, attempt to draw out from the students the range of possible responses to the poster:

- Were there significant differences in attitude between the three main groups: (colonists, settlers, indigenous Australians)?
- Were there differences amongst individuals within the three groups?

Ask the class to select one or two of the most interesting responses:

- In these examples, how have the students symbolized their response using gesture or body language?

The historical context within which the real poster was issued was, of course, extremely complex. For one thing, Van Diemen's Land was a penal colony and many of the people transported there in the early nineteenth century were eventually able to work their 'ticket of leave' which entitled them to settle and acquire land. This inevitably brought them into conflict with the indigenous Australians, for whom the land itself was spiritually and culturally symbolic as well as economically essential.

The pattern of violence between black and white in Van Diemen's Land was fully established by 1815. It went on against a background of proclamations by the lieutenant-governor . . . enjoining the settlers not to provoke or persecute the blacks and stressing that they had the full protection of English law. Their utterances weighed nothing against the reality of invasion: The whites were on the blacks' land, and grabbing as much of it as they could.

Robert Hughes, *The Fatal Shore*

However, there is some evidence that when the first fleet arrived in Australia some 37 years earlier there was no particular ambition on the part of the British to do harm to the indigenous Australians. The first Governor, Phillip, issued proclamations that any settlers who harmed them would be punished and began the penal settlement with the intention of 'reconciling the aboriginals to live amongst us, and to teach them the advantages they will reap from cultivating the land'.

Attitudes obviously hardened quickly. The Aborigines did not want to give up their way of life and resisted attempts to take their land. This in turn caused retaliation, and in time ongoing skirmishes between the two sides developed into brutal conflict. The colonists persecuted them and their superior weapons eventually caused whole groups to be wiped out.

When the colonists landed in Van Diemen's Land in 1804 there were an estimated 4,000 indigenous Australians. By the 1860s – 50 years after the poster was issued – there were no indigenous Australians left in the territory. The last Tasmanian Aborigine died in 1846.

- Was the sentiment expressed in the poster genuinely intended?
- If so, when, and why, did the attitude of the colonists toward the indigenous Australians change?

In groups of five or six, ask the students to create a short scene which attempts to pinpoint a significant moment in the 50-year period during which attitudes changed with such devastating results.

In your groups – using the convention of small-group playmaking – create a short scene which shows a particular event: try to pinpoint something which might have changed the relationship between black and white. Be sure to demonstrate clearly what happens in the scene. Be sure to consider the possible repercussions of the event depicted.

For instance, one group might choose to focus on a particular injustice or mis-understanding which hardens attitudes on both sides; another on a relationship between a black man and white woman – a symbol of peace and integration – which progresses well until someone in authority pronounces it 'unnatural' – with the effect of distancing the two groups. A third might choose to concentrate on the duplicity of the whites: they show the Governor's speech juxtaposed with the 'reality' of his soldiers' brutal treatment of a black family.

Once presented, ask the class to view the scenes as 'theories'– do any of them suggest possible explanations for the historical 'problem'? Perhaps as homework, ask the class to undertake further historical research on the 'real' background to their dramas: which of their 'theories' are supported by the historical evidence? Whilst it is clear that students have produced fictional accounts of possible events, do they feel that using drama as an investigative tool in this way might help to understand the past?

- What might be the pitfalls or problems of 'mixing up' drama and history?
- Can the class think of dramas based on historical events that they have seen?
- Some drama of this type in recent years has proved very controversial – can they give – or find out – examples?
- What do they feel about the notion that history is itself a series of stories – often told by those with power or vested interests?

Stage eight

The final exercises of this unit aim to help students to create a dramatic metaphor which might provide an interesting means of reflecting on the work covered so far.

Remind the group that a metaphor provides a means of thinking about one thing in terms of something else. Ask the class for examples of metaphors. For example:

- *The game of life.*
- *A puppet government.*
- *All the world's a stage.*
- *On a knife edge.*
- *A paper tiger.*
- *Sweeping something under the carpet.*
- *Hair of burnished gold.*

Ask the class to create tableaux or short scenes based around these metaphors – the context can be their own and need not be related to the ongoing drama. They must use the image in the metaphor as part of the work – and not just use the title as a starting point for an improvisation.

The next task is to create a more developed dramatic metaphor – in other words, to show a particular relationship or situation in terms that are not literally true, but nevertheless may express a 'truth'. For instance, the relationship between a teacher and his or her pupils could be shown as:

Van Diemen's Land

- Explorers setting out on a journey.
- A puppeteer pulling the strings.
- A gardener tending prize seedlings.
- A trainer preparing athletes for a race.
- A prison warder and prisoners.

Dramatic metaphors

Playwrights and directors have often created dramas in which a central metaphor is used to unify the drama. We provide a number of examples; can students think of their own – perhaps from film or TV?

Franz Kafka/Steven Berkoff – *Metamorphosis*

Kafka's character is literally transformed into a beetle – which reflects the reality of the middle-class world which he seeks to escape.

J & K Capek – *The Insect Play*

In this play of the 1920s, insects again serve as metaphors which illuminate human desires and conflicts.

Henrik Ibsen – *A Doll's House*

The title provides a metaphor which suggests the themes of power and manipulation developed in the play.

L. Frank Baum's *The Wizard of Oz* contains many metaphors (hundreds!) relating to life as a journey down *The Yellow Brick Road*.

Encourage students to consider the situation within the penal colony on a metaphorical level. The following prompts may help to engage the class' thinking in the 'generalized' terms necessary:

- Who depends on whom? (Convicts, colonists and Aborigines)?
- Whose laws should apply?
- Whose behaviour is the most 'civilized'?
- Who has the most power?
- Who deserves the most power?
- Who has most right to the land?

Ask the students to go back into role – as the convict, colonist or Aborigine that they portrayed in Stage four. Ask each to find a partner – from another 'group'. Once pairs are established ask the students to explore the relationship between the two types of people physically. This can be achieved through the construction of simple tableaux, but can be extended in terms of dramatic action through the use of a sculpting technique. Students can take it in turns to physically manipulate the images created by other pairs: quite subtle changes (a hand on a shoulder; a sideways glance) can produce significant effects.

Do the physical images created suggest possible metaphors that express something of the relationship between these groups? Ask the pairs to develop their work into a deliberate dramatic metaphor that might give an interesting focus to a drama based on transportation.

Metaphorically, could you describe a penal colony as:

- *Hell?*
- *A nest of termites?*
- *A circus?*
- *A village?*
- *A game?*
- *A jungle?*

Can the group make other suggestions?

In the same way, could the relationship between jailers and convicts be:

- *Two sides of a coin?*
- *Lord and servant?*
- *Cat and mouse?*

Could the students create short scenes – which *demonstrate* their ideas by using the metaphor quite literally?

Do the more abstract associations made possible by this approach provide a means to reflect upon the drama as a whole?

The resources for this Unit are available for download at www.routledge.com/ 9780415572064

Persuasion

Thematic content in this unit:

Advertisements and advertising language

Writing to persuade

Marketing and branding

Image and ethics

Curriculum connections:

Media Studies

English, Media Studies

Music, Art & Graphic Design

Vocational Studies, Citizenship, Drama

Dramatic techniques and keywords in this unit:

Mantle of the Expert

Teacher in role

Storyboarding

In this unit, students will explore some aspects of modern advertising and gain an insight into some of the techniques and language employed by this global multi-billion dollar industry. Taking the standpoint that we are all consumers in one form or another, the drama work encourages the students to consider how marketing campaigns and effective product and corporate branding influence our buying habits, and make us behave in certain ways.

The opening drama convention is a simplified form of *Mantle of the Expert;*[1] a whole group role-play led by the teacher in role. In this fictional environment, the students will work in role as advertising 'creatives', whose goal is to secure a new and lucrative account from a high-profile company. Within this drama convention, it is possible to simulate the competitive ethos that perhaps reflects the nature of business and the commercial world – as well as acting as a motivator for less engaged learners. The prize at the end of the creative process for the 'winning' group is being awarded the account. However, in this drama, perhaps all is not as it seems!

There is the opportunity to explore media-specific elements during the work, which could include filming and editing, sound recording or designing print media. Not all school drama departments will have access to the expertise or equipment needed for some of the tasks, so the opportunity to link up with Media or English departments might offer a valid cross-curricular element. In addition, Music and Graphic Design can be explored at different stages during the process of creating the advertising campaign and can be emphasized by the teacher to become significant elements of the students' presentations in role and performances. Needless to say, the drama 'product' created within the unit can stand alone as short performances, or can be captured successfully using very basic video equipment.

Once this project on advertising is completed, the following can be taught in sequence. This would enable students to explore some of the wider ethical questions surrounding manufacture and labour that arise once a product has moved from concept and development into production. It is hoped that this element of the work will act as a thought-provoking contrast to the earlier explorations of competition and consumerism.

Where this unit connects

This unit provides opportunities for learning in a number of curriculum areas. In developing a fictional advertising agency students will explore aspects of advertising, marketing and branding which clearly connects with media studies and elements of vocational learning. As the students are creating and writing material designed to sell a product, there are connections with English and writing to persuade or influence. As the work progresses into the unit on child labour, students will be encouraged to explore social, cultural and ethical issues surrounding workforce exploitation which will inform citizenship and PSHE-based discussion and reflection. The students will employ a range of oral techniques as they plan and present their drama and negotiate working to a set brief collaboratively in a variety of group sizes and combinations.

Working in drama: by the end of this unit students will have:

- Created a series of short prepared improvisations within a dramatic framework based around modern television advertising.

- Interacted with a teacher in role, negotiating and developing the drama in groups.

- Considered the implications of the developing work and made adaptations and changes where necessary.

- Explored how drama and language might be used to persuade and influence others through engagement in a range of practical tasks.

- Had the opportunity to draw connections between the branding and marketing of a particular product and the labour involved in its manufacture.

Section one

Stage one – advertising: how much do you know?

This section introduces some specific advertising terms that should encourage the students into thinking a little more deeply about the specific techniques employed by advertising agencies to sell products. Of course, teachers can choose how much time they wish to spend building this contextual knowledge, but flagging up key terms such as *logo, slogan, brand* etc., often helps secure stronger responses once students are introduced to the advertising brief in the whole group role-play that follows.

Explain that this drama project will explore the world of marketing and advertising, but will first identify some key advertising techniques and how they influence our behaviour as consumers.

Read out or project the following definition:

Advertising is the activity of selling a product, service or an idea by . . .

Form groups of four; issue each group with a pad of sticky notes or paper with a pen for each person. Using a *Rally Robin* (a *Kagan* technique[2] in which each member of the group in turn quickly writes an answer and posts it centrally) ask the group to name as many different forms and types of advertising that they can.

Asking the students to consider the many different places where advertising takes place might help them identify some of the less obvious techniques. For example, a sponsored footballer's shirt, branded shopping bag or hot air balloon or blimp. Stop the groups and share some of the lists.

Broadly speaking, advertising could fall into the following categories:

Broadcast – television, radio and cinema advertising.
Included in this could be product placement in films and programmes or sponsorship by companies for certain shows or series. This links neatly with the origins of radio and later television advertising in the 1940s and 1950s when weekly daytime dramas were created by soap manufactures such as Proctor & Gamble to advertise their products, often through a pause in the broadcast to allow 'a brief message from our sponsors'. In the early days, the drama was little more than a vehicle to engage a viewing public into watching the advertising message, but over time the viewing public became more interested in the characters and weekly ongoing storylines than the adverts. These programmes we now refer to as 'soaps' or 'soap-operas', a reference to the original products that sponsored those 1940s broadcasts.

Print – newspaper and magazine advertisements, brochures or flyers; direct mail catalogues and leaflets; posters; shopping bags.

Outside or site-specific advertising – signs and billboards, screens and displays; bus, tram, train, underground or taxi posters; sandwich boards; van livery and towed moving trailers with displays; retail point-of-sale displays; blimps; banners; flags; balloons.

Internet and web-based advertising – an area that is continuing to find new ways of advertising products. It is estimated that 78 per cent of all emails received are 'spam' and worldwide billions of spam emails are sent daily. As well as this indiscriminate direct marketing approach, the Internet can be used to target groups of individuals very effectively too, for example through sponsored links on search engines or 'pop-ups' on web pages. Some years ago, companies realized that if they created a short, funny or thought-provoking video that raised awareness of their product they could then rely on people sharing that video through their own emails or on social networking or video-sharing sites like *YouTube*. This technique, now known as 'viral marketing', is employed by many of the world's top companies to sell their products.

Stage two – branding

A key part of bringing a product to market is the creation of the *brand* that the consumer then 'buys into'. Companies spend a great deal of money in developing a strong brand image that captures the essence of the product or service and inspires consumer confidence and loyalty. Some companies have kept the same brand for decades, even if the product has evolved or developed or changed completely.

Explain to the students that branding is linked strongly with image. Consumers who 'buy into a brand' are identifying with the values of that product and that decision is supposed to reflect their particular lifestyle choices.

As part of their marketing strategy, some companies use *product endorsement* and sponsorship to link their product with a high profile personality, team or sporting event. Industries attached to sporting products are very likely to use this strategy, where the label or badge that the customer chooses indicates their passion and commitment.

Persuasion

Building a successful brand takes a long time and there are different techniques that companies use to help raise public awareness and build their consumer base.

Slogans

Straplines, endlines and *slogans* are different terms used when a word or catchphrase is attached to the brand or product in order to highlight a feature with which the company wishes to be associated. Usually these slogans are short, memorable phrases, designed to stick in people's memories. Discuss any memorable advertising slogans that the group can bring to mind.

What makes a good slogan?

As a group, ask the students to complete advertising slogans such as these:

'Just …'	(Just Do it)
(Nike)	
'The future's bright …'	(The future's bright, the future's Orange)
(Orange)	
'I'm …'	'(I'm lovin' it)
(McDonald's)	
'Because I'm …'	(Because I'm worth it)
(L'Oréal)	
'The best a man …'	(The best a man can get)
(Gillette)	

There are lists of current and popular slogans on various websites. To show how effective slogans can be in promoting product identity, it is interesting to see if any of the group recognize the product from some of these earlier slogans, despite the campaigns being started many years ago:

'They're grrrrreat'
(Kellogg's Frosties, 1952)
'I liked it so much, I brought the company'
(Remington, 1979)
'Beanz Meanz Heinz'
(Heinz Baked Beans, 1967)

Logos

A logo is a graphic design that identifies a company and it needs to be immediately recognizable by the public. The logo often includes the name of the company or product in a specific typeface, or it might be a design that is symbolic or non-representational. Once a logo has established itself upon the public consciousness it acts as a very effective visual shortcut, with the consumer making the connection between logo, product and what the company stands for in an instant.

Share the following logos with the students: McDonald's, Nike and Apple.

Can they identify the product or company?

What are the design elements that make the logo effective? Consider colour, shape, and simplicity. Is it easy to remember?

Ask the students to get into pairs and sit facing each other. Taking turns and in silence, ask each student to draw a logo for his or her partner to guess. Then swap over; award points to the one who draws the most recognized logos in three minutes!

> The Nike slogan featuring the famous 'swoosh' was created in 1971 by Carolyn Davidson, a graphic design student who was reportedly paid $35 for her design. Davidson was hired by Phil Knight, the founder of Blue Ribbon Sports, to design a logo for a shoe stripe. She based her idea on the wing of a statue of the Greek goddess of victory – Nike. The Nike brand went on to become one of the world's most successful sportswear and equipment manufacturers. In 1983 Davidson was rewarded more fully by a grateful Phil Knight with stocks and shares in the company and a gold ring in the shape of the Nike swoosh.

Jingles and sonic branding

Since the early days of radio and television advertising, the jingle has played an important part in building brand awareness. Companies have found that lyrics about the product set to memorable music help the audience recall the brand much better than words alone. Like logos, some very early jingles have stood the test of time and are still used today. More recently, the phenomenon of sonic branding has seen jingles develop into very short tonal melodies that have no words. These tunes are sometimes only four or five notes long and are the aural equivalent of the visual logo, attempting to capture the essence of the product or company in a few seconds of sound. Famous examples of sonic brands are Intel's four note 'bongs', McDonald's' 'I'm Lovin' It' refrain, and the Microsoft Windows 'start up' tune.

Ask the students if they can hum the tune. Can they think of any other successful jingles and sonic brands?

Sonic branding

This exercise will explore the way sonic branding or *audio identity* attempts to capture the essence of a product or company in just a few seconds of recorded sound. Sound logos are easily remembered by the customer and often trigger an emotional response, acting as a short cut to make the consumer think about a particular brand.

Task: research the following sonic branding examples:

- Pearl and Dean's *Asteroid*
- McDonald's' *Lovin' it*
- THX's *Deep Note*

- Dolby Sound trailer

- X Box 360

- Microsoft's and Apple's *start up sound*

- Direct Line's *bugle fanfare*

- Intel's *Bongs*

- Any of the BBC's, ITV's or Channel Four's series of 'idents'.

It can take months to compose even a few seconds of music that identifies the brand effectively and there are specialized companies that aim to provide that service. Find some websites and see what they offer, and how they go about providing creative solutions for their clients.

Working in a pair, start by choosing a car, perfume or sportswear brand that you are familiar with. These sorts of products often have 'attitude' and rely on their customers making a personal statement by 'buying into' the brand.

Using a music keyboard, you are going to design a sonic logo that matches your brand. Remember the sound should capture in some way the key ways the brand wants to be perceived by the customer, so start by making a list of five words or 'identities' that you think sums up the brand. These could be words like: *playful, a winner, technology, serious, youthful, challenging, new, inspirational, entertaining, professional, advanced, stylish, down to earth, delicate, robust, strong, old fashioned, beautiful.*

Begin to compose your sound logo and remember you cannot include words in your final piece. Think about the melody – the actual sequence of notes or chords and the range between those notes; are they close together in the high, medium or low range or do they move significantly from very low to very high? Are you going to employ harmonies? Harmonies are created when notes and chords are played together. Some harmonies are consonant and some dissonant. Consonant harmonies usually create a sense of peace and stability, whereas dissonant harmonies can create tension and unease – because it sounds like the notes are 'clashing'.

Think about tonal qualities and your choice of 'voice' or instrument and explore rhythm by experimenting with accented beats and different tempo or pace. Don't forget that modern keyboards often have effects such as echo and sustain which can add a very different quality to your composition. Decide if your sound logo builds in volume and intensity to a crescendo or fades to a decrescendo.

Your sonic logo should only last a few seconds, it has to be memorable and for the purposes of this exercise certainly less than 15 seconds. Your final product may only contain a handful of notes or chords, but has been designed to reflect your chosen brand and the qualities you associated with it.

You can record your final piece, or play it live in a group sharing of the work. Be prepared to discuss all the choices you made during the composition.

Section two – the advertising agency

Stage one – the brief

Explain to the students that this drama project will involve working in role as members of an advertising agency. They will be responding to an advertising brief and be expected to present their ideas within the context of working collaboratively to complete a project. Explain that there are many different roles within an advertising agency, but that we will be focusing upon the 'creatives'; the people who design and create advertising campaigns. Explain that you will take on the role of the Chief Accounts Manager who is the link between the client (in this case a manufacturer) and the agency.

Ask for some suggestions for the name of the agency from the group and write up or project the successful idea.

Gather the students into a circle and explain that you are going to introduce the work in role.

- **Who are we?**   Adults who work as *creatives* in an advertising agency.
- **Where are we?**   In the agency's conference room.
- **When are we?**   Present day.

Welcome to this morning's briefing. I apologize for taking you away from your other projects, but the agency has an opportunity to land a very big account with a multi-million pound sports equipment and sportswear client and I need the best creative minds from the agency working with me on this one.

At this point hand out or project the *creative brief*:

Creative brief – memory material sports shoes

What is it?

Scientists working on an international space programme have developed a new polymer material unlike any other. The material (chemical name *amorphospolymoxturane*) has the feel and properties of leather but is both *adaptive* and *intelligent*. The 'unique selling proposition' (USP) of this material is simple but amazing: When a small electrical charge is introduced, the fabric is able to learn to mould around any shape and create a soft, supportive and extremely comfortable second skin.

Our client, *MP (Memorypolymer) Incorporated* has won the exclusive rights to use this material and intends to take it to market in the form of a technologically superior sports training shoe. It is set to revolutionize the sports footwear industry. We have the chance to create the brand identity of the product and launch a major print media and broadcast advertising campaign.

Who are we talking to?

The customers for the trainer are young 15–27, fashion conscious, cutting-edge men and women. They will expect to pay a premium to have the best products and shop in the more expensive stores. Most will take part in sports, gym or outdoor leisure activities at least once a week. Our customers associate themselves with premium brands and high profile teams and individuals; many of them will compete at some level, and see themselves as winners and leaders. They will invariably have computer access (spending on average 46 minutes a day online) and be technological aware and connected via social networking sites, like *Twitter* and email.

Why do we need advertising?

We need to make sure this product becomes the next 'must have'. Customers must have complete confidence that they are buying into a product that reflects their high sporting standards, but is still stylish and fashionable. We want to build a long-term relationship with our customer base and inspire their lasting brand loyalty.

What do we need?

Initially we need:
- A brand name for the **material** and the **trainer**.

- A slogan.

- A logo.

Spend some time working as a whole group discussing the brief. Identify the students' initial ideas about the potential customers; what sort of *price point* do they think the trainer might *retail* for; any initial ideas or concepts?

Identifying the 'unique selling proposition' or USP of the product should be the starting point of this task as well as deciding whether to create a name that is descriptive or invented. Remind the groups that brand names are protected, so they cannot use an existing product and would not want their creation to be associated with a rival anyway. Experimenting with language, combinations of words and arrangements of letters can be an interesting starting point.

> ### *Mantle of the Expert* – building belief
>
> In the opening stages of *Mantle of the Expert* dramas, students normally assume *functional roles* – that is, they are largely defined by their particular expertise, in this case as 'creatives' working within an advertising agency. However, as the drama develops, roles often become more differentiated; students are often keen to demonstrate that *their* 'creative' has a particular attribute or strength, and as long as this does not become obtrusive, it can contribute a sense of developing belief in the work.
>
> There are also a number of exercises that could be included in the drama to help build belief in the enterprise in a similar way. For example:
>
> **Coffee Mugs**: this advertising agency provides regular coffee breaks! Ask the students to design the coffee mug that their character has brought to work to use. What does the mug say about the person and their role within the team?
>
> **Car Park**: provide a plan of the advertising agency's car park – with designated parking slots sketched in. Ask the students to enter a description of 'their' car – and its registration plate – into 'their' parking space.
>
> This exercise is particularly interesting to use in hierachical enterprises!

Stage two – the pitch

Now explain that they will be working in groups of four or five and that initially they are in competition with each other to come up with the most imaginative – but realistic – response to the brief. Explain that deadlines are important (*in business!*) and as such they will only have 20 minutes to prepare, before they present their responses to you – the Chief Accounts Manager – and the rest of the agency.

Provide some large A3 pieces of paper and pens and ask the group to brainstorm their initial ideas.

Remind them that the task has two elements; the ideas stage and then the pitch itself. Remind the group that as professionals they are expected to produce a polished and well-rehearsed two minute pitch that details their ideas – and the thinking behind them. Groups might like to consider creating flash-cards or graphics on paper that will support their ideas. Explain that only the best ideas will be taken forward to the next phase of the campaign, so groups should attempt to keep their work secret until their presentation.

Allow groups time to develop their ideas. Visiting each in role as the high-status Chief Accounts Manager helps to maintain authenticity and build belief – and can help sustain a healthy work rate. Ten minutes into the task, remind them that they need to have made their decisions and begin to practise their presentation.

At the end of the working time re-arrange the room so there is a clear performance area. If necessary re-establish the context of the advertising agency and remind the students that during each pitch there are no comments, but that *colleagues will have a chance to discuss all the presentations at the end of the process.*

Invite each group to present their pitch. At the end of the sharing, spend some time discussing the strengths of each idea. Negatives should, as usual, be handled in a positive way, but remind all groups that they should see each stage of the development process as an opportunity to evaluate and improve their own creative ideas.

Mantle of the Expert – developing expertise through doing

In the classic *Mantle of the Expert* drama (see introduction) as originally outlined by Dorothy Heathcote, things take time to develop; in the book *Drama for Learning*,[3] written with Gavin Bolton, there are accounts of classroom dramas that are sustained over many weeks – even months – of work.

Heathcote has described the way that students 'grow into' their expertise through working together on focused tasks. In much of her work the fictional 'agency' – for which the students work, and which provides a collaborative enterprise for the group as they co-operate as part of a like-minded community – is engaged in minor tasks before coming to the main focus of the drama; in this way students have the chance to *assume* the mantle of expertise, and as Heathcote comments, to pick up the 'action' at a point of significance.

However, developing work at this level of detail is not always possible. Teachers – like everyone else in the modern world – are pressured for time; sometimes compromises need to be made.

In this unit we have attempted to provide a framework based upon *Mantle of the Expert* that can be taught realistically in the time slots normally available for drama in UK secondary schools. If time allows, however, teachers could fruitfully set up the frame of the advertising agency in advance of the arrival of the *MP Incorporated* contract, and work through smaller-scale tasks – for different 'clients' – first. This strategy helps to establish more of the 'history' of the agency – which Heathcote suggests can help students build belief in the situation, in their own ability to undertake complex tasks, and help them to develop the sense of responsibility and care which comes through doing a good job.

Stage three – the poster

Address the students in role, congratulating them on their work so far, and introduce the next task.

I'd like to see how some of these ideas would stand up in an initial outdoor sites poster campaign. What would your poster for this campaign look like? Return to your groups and create a still image that captures your ideas. I want you to include the slogan, and brand name too, as spoken words. You should experiment with different ways of saying those words: perhaps one person speaking solo; perhaps as a group, chorally.

Remember that most outdoor poster sites are in places of high volume passing traffic or pedestrian footfall. Potential customers will only see your poster for a few seconds so it has to be visually striking and engaging. In 10 minutes we share your ideas.

Now, what makes a good poster image?

Allow some whole group discussion time to discuss good examples of posters; how a single image can convey a narrative; how they might physically represent something more abstract, and how their slogan and brand name will link to their chosen image.

Set the groups to work and allow appropriate working time.

Before stopping the preparation work, go to each group and assign their performance space and create an order for sharing the poster presentations. Initially ask all the students to get into position and explain that they are going to present their images all at the same time. Quickly inspect all the images, before explaining that each group will now recreate their image individually. Explain that as you draw level with each group, they should quickly get into position and hold their image for 10 seconds before you move onto the next group. Again remind the students that as professionals there should be no comment between each group's performance and there will be plenty of time to discuss ideas at the end. Once the group is settled, share the work in this manner then draw the whole group into a circle and evaluate.

Stage four – the television advertisement

This is the final phase of the advertising work and results in the students creating their own 30-second television commercial promoting their product. In role, explain that the client has been excited by the responses of the group and wants to take the process to its logical conclusion: a television advertisement.

Explain that the advert need not be related to the previous poster so that groups have the freedom to pursue a different approach. It can be helpful to lead into this work by showing some current, famous or particularly successful advertisements. There are lots of websites dedicated to sharing adverts and a web search should offer numerous examples.

Some of the most popular and memorable advertisements use humour to sell the product; ask students if they think that the brief they are working to would benefit from using humour – or is their product more orientated towards a 'serious' approach?

Point out that some advertisements have a clear narrative and tell a story whereas some are more abstract in form. Again, a brief discussion with examples may be useful to the students before they move into the planning phase.

Ask the groups to re-form and explain that the next 10 minutes will be dedicated to developing the concept for the advert. Ask the groups to look again at the creative brief, and reiterate the type of person that the advertising is seeking to engage.

The groups will need large sheets of paper and pens to record their responses and create mind maps and brainstorms.

Assign roles – Art Director, copywriter, etc., and after sufficient time stop the work. If the groups have arrived at a *concept* they can now move on to the next step – which is *storyboarding* and *scripting*.

Scripting and writing to persuade

A *copywriter* composes the language of advertising, be it the words on a poster or the script of a TV advertisement. In both instances it is about persuading the consumer to adopt the product's values and then actually do something about it. In marketing this is often called the 'call to action' and is the instruction you want the reader or viewer to actually do – *buy these shoes* or *phone this number,* for example. Often in TV advertising, the 'call to action' is implicit rather than overtly stated; *if you identify with these smart people, you'll wear these clothes or drive this brand of car.*

Task: write your script for the 'copy' in your television advertisement. Remember that this includes any voice-overs or titles in the advert as well as any dialogue between actors. Read through these instructions to help you.

Effective copywriting to persuade will take account of the audience, the purpose and the genre or tone of the advert. Here are some tips to ensure imaginative and effective copy.

- Know your product and state its benefits – what will the customer get in return for buying them?
- Use language that your audience will know and relate to;
  - Use 'You' rather than 'We';
  - Avoid too much information – keeping your message simple makes it more memorable;
  - Do not lie – avoid statements that could be proved wrong. You cannot say a product is the 'best in the world', unless you can prove it.
- Be wary of comparing your product with others, you might be inadvertently introducing a rival and you might get sued by them!

Briefly explain that storyboarding is a technique whereby a piece of moving film or television is broken down into a series of pictures displayed in sequence that tell the story. Often the images correspond to a different camera shot or angle, and seen together it is easy to visualize what the finished film will look like. The images themselves do not have to be sophisticated; they can be simple line drawings. There are lots of examples to be seen on the Internet that could be projected or photocopied for students' reference. Comic strips and graphic novels also offer good examples of storytelling through pictures.

Provide sheets of A3 paper for each group. Folding the paper along its longest edge and then in half and in half again along its shorter edge will divide up the paper into a landscape series of eight cells on which to work. Ask the students to label each box in sequence, top left to bottom right, and to begin to complete their storyboard, starting with their opening or *establishing shot* in cell one. Encourage the students to include any relevant descriptions, lines of text or graphics in the boxes along with the images.

Once the students have completed their storyboards, explain that they will translate their storyboard into a series of still images that they will perform. They can use only the language they have written on the storyboard, but they can include a narrator who will briefly title each image. For this task students cannot include any movement other than the transitions between the images. Allow 10 minutes for this task and share the work.

Once the work has been shared and discussed, explain that each commercial will be 'mocked up' for the client, either as a live performance of the complete 30 seconds sequence, or a filmed sequence. The groups will need some more planning time to move their storyboard of still images into a complete piece of work. Explain that any graphics can be presented on sheets of paper, or added later in the editing phase if the work is being recorded on video. Allow time for the students to prepare their work before creating a formal performance space and inviting each group to share their work.

Discuss and evaluate the work. Inform the group that, as the Account Manager, you are required to recommend one idea to the client. However, as the work is so strong you are going to present all the ideas and let the client decide which campaign will be produced.

Stage five – the showdown

Present the following 'email':

Dear (name of agency chosen earlier by students),

MP
MEMORYPOLYMER
INCORPORATED

Re: New sports shoe range

We have been sent the rough edits of the TV ads you have been working on – and I have to say, we are *very* impressed.

We see this product becoming a global brand, and plan to move it into production as soon as possible. Due to the high cost of the intelligent memory material the trainers are made from, we have had to look at production costs very carefully. As a result we have just negotiated an amazing deal with factories in India and China, of course this is a sensitive issue in the world's media so can I pledge you all to secrecy until the contracts are signed? There are too many 'do-gooders' out there who just don't understand how business works.

This could be a big opportunity for us all: will you work with us to develop the product further?

Looking forward to working with you in the next phase of the project – and making lots of money!

John B. Stuart
Managing Director
MP (Memorypolymer) Incorporated

Persuasion

Ask for the creatives' response to the email from John B. Stuart of *MP Inc.*

- Is there anything they find surprising or interesting about the email?
- Why does MP (Memorypolymer) Incorporated seem to be anxious to keep their plans to base their production abroad a secret?
- Is it any business of the advertising agency, how or where the product is actually made? After all, they just help sell the product.

Some time later, the advertising agency team get another message (this could be in the form of an email, text, or even straight-to-camera video footage). This anonymous message comes from someone in one of the countries where the shoes are to be made:

I have heard that you are working for MP Inc. on their new product. I thought you might like to know a few things about how they get their shoes made.

In this factory the shoes are made by children. Some of them work on machines that stamp out the hard rubber sole. The machines don't have proper guards on them. The youngest children sit on the floor and stitch the logo onto the shoe. Some of them are six years old and they get paid a few rupees for each one they do. The day lasts for 12 hours and if anyone complains they get beaten and lose their job. All the children should be in school, but they cannot afford to go, they all must work to contribute to their families . . .

This is why your trainers can be made so cheaply over here. This is why they can keep their costs so low.

Gather the students, and again gauge their reaction to the message.

At this stage in the drama there are a number of choices available:

1 The advertising agency can confront John B. Stuart from MP Inc. with the whistleblower's message.

2 The drama is taken to a further stage by a piece of narration: *the creative team went off abroad to research locations for the next phase of the work. Whilst they were there, they decided to find out as much as they could about* **Memorypolymer Incorporated** *and their manufacturing plant . . .*

This option involves students 'researching' by interviewing children who work at the MP Inc. factory (simple role-play in pairs), and returning to present their findings (as video footage of the 'edited' interviews).

There are thousands of websites and publications that explore the complex issues surrounding child labour. We recommend students carry out their own research focusing on established organizations such as Save the Children and UNICEF to begin to gather facts and case studies that will inform their opinions.

3 You can link this drama with the next unit in this book, *Child Labour*. Focusing particularly on the later sections will provide students with opportunities to explore this morally complex series of issues in more depth.

4 Whatever option is chosen the drama will need some form of resolution. We have found that a 'confrontation' where the *creatives* meet with the boss of MP Inc, provides students with an opportunity to present their objections, demonstrate their knowledge of the topic and also show their ability to 'persuade'. As such, it can present a useful 'synoptic' assessment opportunity!

Students can help plan the final encounter, which could include:

- Presentation of the 'evidence' – presented, of course, in drama form, as documentary footage, filmed interviews or personal testimony to a representative of MP Inc.

- A section where John B. Stuart accuses the team of naivety, and attempts to persuade them to complete their lucrative advertising work.

- Discussion with Mr Stuart threatening to award the advertising contract to another company, leading to a moment of decision: will the students withdraw from the contract? ... *after all, there are plenty more agencies out there who would be glad of the work ...*

- A moment of resolution where the agency either withdraws from the contract, forcing an indignant and angry goodbye (... *you'll be hearing from my lawyers!*), or a morally dubious reconciliation.

- An (out of role) plenary that gives students the opportunity to reflect upon the choices made in the drama, and their implications.

The resources for this Unit are available for download at www.routledge.com/ 9780415572064

Child labour

Thematic content in this unit:	Curriculum connections:
Child labour: the rights of children	History
Perceptions of childhood and family life	English, History
Poverty in the historical and contemporary world	History, Geography, PSHE
Global ethical and cultural citizenship	Geography, Citizenship, PSHE
The rights and responsibilities of employers and their employees	History, Citizenship
The Industrial Revolution, life in the workhouse, mines and cotton mills	History
Folk tunes and popular culture – exploring, recording and celebrating the past	History, Music
The responsibilities of consumers	Media Studies, Citizenship

Dramatic techniques and keywords in this unit:

Hot-seating	Teacher in role	Mime
Tableau	Narration and self-narration	Montage

This unit explores the topic of child labour and the rights of children. By contrasting the experience of young people today with the lives of children 200 years ago, the teaching activities hope to pose ethical questions about exploitation from a global context, as well as help students to explore some of the laws and strategies designed to protect children. By utilizing a global perspective it is hoped that students will discover that the issues surrounding child labour are rarely simple.

Where this unit connects

Childhood, as we recognize it today in the developed countries of the G8, is a relatively modern concept. Education, human rights and an expectation not to be exploited are identified in law. This unit is designed to raise awareness of where some of those rights have come from, and how a person's experience of childhood radically differs depending on where in the world they live. Fittingly, as the unit is about people's experiences, it has personal testimony and real-life narrative at its core. Based on the recorded accounts of workers and their masters, the drama opens by exploring the experience of a group of *pauper apprentices*, sent from London to Nottingham to work in the cotton mills of the Industrial Revolution. Using diary accounts, and an exploration of how a modern folk song has interpreted one young person's life, students can consider connections between what is happening today – to millions of children and their families, caught in a cycle of poverty – with what happened in the United Kingdom 200 years ago.

Working in drama: by the end of this unit students will have:

● Compared present day ideas of childhood with historical testimony of children from the Industrial Revolution and accounts of modern children in emerging economies and developing countries.

● Employed a variety of strategies including hot-seating, improvisation and mime to create characters and present drama based on historical evidence and testimony.

● Explored some of the techniques of political theatre to create drama seeking to effect change.

Section one

Stage one

Gather the students and explain that the drama work will start straight away with an individual task, exploring the word childhood. Ask the students to find a space where they can stand or sit alone and think of one thing they associate with childhood and being a child. Some suggestions might be playground games, friendships, presents, birthdays, Christmas or other religious festivals and celebrations, school or holidays. Encouraging students to focus on a specific activity, rather than an abstract quality will help some students for the next task.

Now tell each of them to find a word or phrase to title that aspect of childhood. It could, for instance, be a line from a nursery rhyme or game. Explain we will be using the technique of *montage*[1] where we will shape a moving frieze of images and sounds with the title *Childhood*. Ask the students to develop a simple gesture or movement that will complement their word.

Allow time to prepare, and then share the work: with the students sitting or standing in position in their own space, invite them to share their work one after the other.

Child labour

If we were preparing a play called 'Childhood', and this was our prologue or opening scene, how might we best develop our work?

Suggestions might be building up the montage one actor at a time with each student entering the empty performance space and repeating their movement motif and language, or everyone entering the space together, creating a group tableau and then starting the movement sequence in unison.

Once the group has had an opportunity to present their work lead a brief discussion remarking on some of the features of childhood they have identified. Were their responses largely positive? Were there any commonalities? Were there any significantly negative images shown?

Finally, were there any students who showed children *at work*?

Stage two

Place the students into pairs and explain that this part of the drama will introduce some of the types of work that children have done in the past. Present the resource sheet – which includes an account of a child *bird scarer*, a *climbing boy* (chimney sweep) and a street *watercress seller*.

Victorian child labour resource sheet

Figure 4.1 Bird Scaring: March, Sir George Clausen, 1896

Source: http://www.mylearning.org/image-zoom.asp?jpageid=3213&picid=1

AWA' birds, away!
Take a little, and leave a little,
And do not come again;
For if you do,
I will shoot you through,
And there is an end of you.

William Arnold aged 6, Northamptonshire, 1860:

When I was six and two months old I was sent off to work. I do not think I shall ever forget those long and hungry days in the fields scaring crows. You can imagine the feeling of loneliness. Hours and hours pass without a living creature coming near. I cried most of the time and in desperation I would shout as loud as I could, 'Mother, mother, mother'. But mother could not hear. She was working in a hayfield two miles away.

BBC Television: *Children of the Revolution*, broadcast date: 11 February 2011

Figure 4.2 The Climbing Boy

The Chimney Sweeper from *Songs of Innocence* by William Blake (1789)

When my mother died I was very young,
And my father sold me while yet my tongue
Could scarcely cry ''weep! 'weep! 'weep! 'weep!'
So your chimneys I sweep & in soot I sleep.

I was presented to the chimney with the grate still hot from the fire latterly extinguished. I was given my iron scrapper and brush and encouraged to enter the narrow flue. I extended one arm above my head and kept my other tight by my side and using my elbows, raised myself upwards until I could gain further purchase by jamming my knees and heels against the rough sides. In this manner I could make slow progress some ten feet or more upwards. At once a panic gripped me and I began to yell for help for fear of being trapped. My master shouted from below that he was to light a fire if I called again. The fear of the smoke and heat rising was enough to encourage me to further efforts and I rapidly ascended the chimney.

Figure 4.3 The Watercress seller

Source: http://www.heritage-images.com/Preview/PreviewPage.aspx?id=1155276&pricing=true&licenseType=RM

I go about the streets with water-creases, crying, "Four bunches a penny, water-creases." I am just eight years old – that's all, and I've a big sister, and a brother and a sister younger than I am. On and off, I've been very near a twelvemonth in the streets … It's very cold before winter comes on reg'lar – specially getting up of a morning. I gets up in the dark by the light of the lamp in the court. When the snow is on the ground, there's no creases. I bears the cold – you must; so I puts my hands under my shawl, though it hurts 'em to take hold of the creases, especially when we takes 'em to the pump to wash 'em.[2]

Ask the pairs to select one account to work on and divide the pairs into A and B. Explain that As will create a series of still images of the child at work and Bs will become the voice of the child narrating the action just using the language available on the resource sheet. Groups that feel restricted by working in still image might like to move the work into dramatic action such as a mimed sequence.

Allow working time, and then share the pair work *in situ* quickly focusing on each pair in the room.

Discuss the performances and ask the group if they can identify the historical period when children undertook these jobs.

Explain that the work will continue by looking at the experience of children prior to the Victorian era who had been placed in the *workhouse*.

Historical sources

This unit has a number of historical *sources* as starting points for the drama. A source is something that tells us about the past. It could take the form of an object or artefact, a document like a letter or newspaper, a photograph or a painting, even a poem or a story can be a historical source. There are two main types of historical sources – *primary sources* and *secondary sources*.

A primary source is one that comes from the past at the time of the event, whereas a secondary source was created later, after the event.

Task: look at the three sources on the worksheet. For each of them, identify whether you think they are primary or secondary sources.

Now decide if you think the source has a particular *bias*? Bias means having an unfair or unbalanced opinion. Secondary sources might well have a bias, as they were produced after the event and might be an attempt to present a particular version of events. However, some primary sources can be biased, too, as people naturally put their feelings into what they write or record. Historians will try to take into account any bias they think is present as they interpret the source.

Look again at the oil painting of 1896 by Sir George Clausen called *Bird Scaring: March*. Look carefully at the expression on the child's face and the position of his hands and feet. What sort of message about the situation of the boy is the artist trying to capture or convey to the viewer? Do you think this piece of evidence is biased?

Section two – the workhouse and the pauper apprentices

Stage one

Display the date *1820* and explain that in that year, 40 per cent of the population in the UK were under 15 years old and the majority of those children were sent to work. For most working class families, children had to work to contribute to the family income. For the thousands of orphans who had no family to look after them, the *workhouse* offered food and shelter from the dangers of living on the streets.

Quickly mind map 'workhouses' and share group knowledge, before continuing.

Workhouses were designed to be harsh in order to deter any but the most desperate of people, and once in the workhouse the orphans lost many of their rights and could be forcibly *apprenticed*. This meant being sold off to factories and businesses as workers. As the Industrial Revolution gathered pace, the cotton mills and textile factories – which were often located in remote areas – needed cheap, accessible labour, so thousands of children from the workhouses were sent to operate their machines and become *pauper apprentices*. Read out the following statement taken from mill owner George Courtauld:

I have eight children coming from Islington on Tuesday next and eight or ten more on Thursday. I had my choice from upwards of 50 girls of different ages and accepted all but one that were within the age of 10 and thirteen. They are from a very well-conducted workhouse and I really expect and earnestly hope that by continued care and attention my establishment of apprentices will prove a nursery of respectable young women fitted for any of the humble walks of life.[3]

Explain to the group that they will be working as a whole group to explore the experience of the pauper apprentices, that you will be acting as a narrator and they are to listen carefully to the story as they will later be enacting parts of it.

Our story begins in a workhouse in St Pancras, London. The year is 1799 and the workhouse is home to around 120 men, women and children. The workhouse provides food and shelter for the poor, helpless and orphans of the area. In return the inmates are set to hard work and have to obey strict rules and face harsh punishments if they break the rules. Conditions in the workhouse are brutal.

Now split the group – girls and boys on opposite sides of the room. Ask them to sit in their own space.

The children would work long hours in the process of oakum picking. Thick, old hemp ship ropes were unravelled and unpicked fibre-by-fibre to create bags of oakum. No tools were used and the rough fibres irritated and infected the skin, making the work extremely painful.

Ask the students to mime unpicking strands of rope as you continue with the story.

The bags of oakum were sold to the navy and ship builders who would mix the fibres with tar and seal the inside of ships (caulking), hence the expression 'money for old rope'.

In the summer of 1799 a rumour circulated that there was going to be an agreement between the churchwardens and the overseers of St Pancras Workhouse, and the owner of a great cotton mill, near Nottingham. The children were told that when they arrived at the cotton mill, they would be transformed into ladies and gentlemen: that they would be fed on roast beef and plum pudding, be allowed to ride their masters' horses, and have silver watches, and plenty of cash in their pockets.

Ask the students to quickly form into pairs. Tell them that the overseer has stepped out of the room. Allow them the chance to talk about the rumour. Do they believe it? How will the children be chosen? Do they want to go?

Add dramatic tension by reminding them that they must not be overheard – they are supposed to be working!

Allow only a few minutes, and share some of the improvisations, before continuing the narrative.

In August of that year, 80 boys and girls who were seven or eight made the 120-mile journey to Nottingham to become parish apprentices in a cotton mill.

The journey was long. As the children got nearer to their destination, they dreamt about what the mill would be like and their imaginations began to conjure up more and more fantastic ideas of their new life as apprentices.

Split the group into pairs. Ask one student in each pair to lead their partner on a 'guided tour' based upon their imaginings of the new apprentice house and mill. They describe the sights, sounds and smells they imagined as they physically lead their partner – who has eyes closed – around the 'mill'. Remind the group that these children were only seven or eight years old and saw the mill as an escape from the drudgery of the workhouse. The guide could focus on the lovely food they will have, the new clothes and shoes they will be given, the rooms and comfy beds they will sleep in, the leisure times and holidays they will have and the money they will earn. If necessary offer the following starting point;

In front of you is a large staircase leading to the dining hall. The smell of roast beef is mouthwatering. The welcoming Master invites you all to sit . . .

Start all the work at the same time and allow a few minutes for the students to complete their 'journey'. *Spotlighting* one or two moments from each one will add dramatic contrast to the reality. Read out Robert Blincoe's account of arriving at the mill:

The young strangers were conducted into a spacious room with long, narrow tables, and wooden benches. They were ordered to sit down at these tables – the boys and girls apart. The supper set before them consisted of milk porridge, of a very blue complexion! The bread was partly made of rye, very black, and so soft, they could scarcely swallow it, as it stuck to their teeth. Where is our roast beef and plum-pudding . . .?[4] (Image from http://www.spartacus.schoolnet.co.uk/IRworkhouse.children.htm.)

Explain to the group that once the children had made their sign on their apprentice deeds, they became the property of the mill owner and would be lodged in the Apprentice House. Typically they would work at the mill until they were 21 or even 24 years old, working six days a week for anything up to 15 hours a day.

Child labour

The younger children were mainly used as *scavengers* or *piecers*. Scavengers would have to crawl underneath enormous moving machines called mules, picking up drifts of loose cotton and wiping down the machinery. Piecers would lean over the working machines and join together the delicate threads of cotton that had snapped.

The task first allocated to Robert Blincoe was to pick up the loose cotton that fell upon the floor. Apparently, nothing could be easier ... although he was much terrified by the whirling motion and noise of the machinery. He also disliked the dust and the flue with which he was half suffocated. He soon felt sick, and by constantly stooping, his back ached. Blincoe, therefore, took the liberty to sit down; but this, he soon found, was strictly forbidden in cotton mills. His overlooker, Mr Smith, told him he must keep on his legs.

John Brown wrote about Robert Blincoe's experiences in a textile mill in an article for *The Lion* newspaper (15 January 1828).[5]

The children could expect to:

- Work for between 15 and 12 hours a day, six days a week, often rising at five in the morning and not finishing till eight or nine at night. Sundays were often spent cleaning down the machines. There might be one hour of schooling a week.

- Stand all day on the factory floor, without sitting down even for mealtimes.

- Eat a poor diet of mainly porridge supplemented with vegetables from the mill garden.

- Work with or crawl under dangerous moving machinery that was deafeningly loud, breathing in air that was hot and humid and thick with cotton dust.

- Suffer terribly with bad backs and aching limbs, eye and breathing problems.

- Be the victims of accidents and even deaths – especially in the last two hours of the shift when the children were most tired.

- Face harsh punishments for being slow or falling asleep. These could be being dunked head first in a barrel of water or hit or beaten with sticks by their overseer. If a girl was caught talking to a boy, she might have her hair shaved off.

Keeping the students in their pairs from the previous exercise, ask them to prepare a duologue based on their dream of what their new life would be like, contrasted with the reality, for example:

We were told to expect roast beef ... but we were served watery porridge.

We thought we'd be able to play ... but we had to work all through the day.

We expected to be treated well ... but the overseers were cruel and we were beaten and punished.

After sufficient preparation time, perform each duologue across the space. Projecting images of children at work in the mills and playing appropriate music to underscore the language will enhance the mood and tension of the drama.

Finish the work and evaluate the performances before moving on to the next section.

Section three – the testimony of Patience Kershaw

Stage one

Explain that this part of the drama will look at another industry that used children in its workforce and will begin with the group *hot-seating* a child from 1841 and that you will be taking on her role. Tell the group that the child is a 17-year-old called Patience Kershaw, and, like the mill workers, her experience of childhood is very different to that of a modern teenager.

During the hot-seating, the group will also be working in role: they will make up a committee of adults who have been charged with looking at conditions of children working in the mines during the 1840s.

> **Lord Ashley**
>
> Anthony Ashley Cooper was the eldest son of the 6th Earl of Shaftesbury. After becoming a Member of Parliament, he turned his attention towards improving the plight of children and particularly those engaged in dangerous or hazardous work mills and factories. Following successful Acts that restricted the age and working hours of children, Lord Ashley turned his reforming gaze towards the unregulated mines and collieries and the Ashley Mining Commission of 1841 was set up to interview hundreds of children and give them the opportunity to describe their daily working experiences.
>
> The subsequent report shocked the nation who, for the main part, had no idea that children and particularly girls and women worked underground in such dangerous conditions. A year after the report, The Mining Act of 1842 was passed which introduced laws restricting children and women from working underground in the mines.

Place an empty chair in the circle and explain that when you sit down you will be in role as Patience. A role signifier such as a simple shawl or piece of cloth held in your hands can be an effective tool to help 'sign' the role. Patience's words are freely available on the Internet and should be photocopied or printed and read out.

Child labour

> ### The testimony of Patience Kershaw aged 17
>
> *Good afternoon ladies and gentlemen. I have written down some of the things that you wanted to know and if you'll let me, I can read my testimony to you now.*
> *My father has been dead about a year; my mother is living and has ten children, five lads and five lasses; the oldest is about 30, the youngest is four; three lasses go to mill; all the lads are colliers, two getters and three hurriers; one lives at home and does nothing; mother does nought but look after home.*
>
> *All my sisters have been hurriers, but three went to the mill. Alice went because her legs swelled from hurrying in cold water when she was hot. I never went to day-school; I go to Sunday-school, but I cannot read or write; I go to pit at five o'clock in the morning and come out at five in the evening; I get my breakfast of porridge and milk first; I take my dinner with me, a cake, and eat it as I go; I do not stop or rest any time for the purpose; I get nothing else until I get home, and then have potatoes and meat, not every day meat. I hurry in the clothes I have now got on, trousers and ragged jacket; the bald place upon my head is made by thrusting the corves; my legs have never swelled, but sisters' did when they went to mill; I hurry the corves a mile and more under ground and back; they weigh 300 cwt.; I hurry 11 a-day; I wear a belt and chain at the workings, to get the corves out; the getters that I work for are naked except their caps; they pull off all their clothes; I see them at work when I go up; sometimes they beat me, if I am not quick enough, with their hands; they strike me upon my back; the boys take liberties with me sometimes they pull me about; I am the only girl in the pit; there are about 20 boys and 15 men; all the men are naked; I would rather work in mill than in coal-pit.*
>
> *There. Now you know. I was told you may wish to ask me some questions?*

Conduct the hot-seating session without coming out of role. Some of the key aspects you might wish to get across are:

A *hurrier* would push (a thruster) or pull the *corves* (tubs or baskets full of coal) from the *coal face*, through the narrow tunnels of the mine. They would often work long shifts in very narrow tunnels. *300 cwt* is the equivalent of around 150 kg.

Check for understanding: what have the students learnt of Patience and her situation?

The students may wish to know why Patience doesn't simply stop working down the mine. The truth for many of these workers was that they had little choice; families had to work in order to earn enough money to survive. As a result there was no time for school, except perhaps a few hours on Sunday.

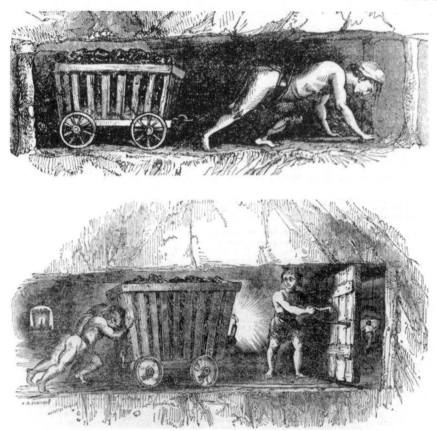

Figure 4.4 Mining images

Source: Illustration from the Report of the 1842 Royal Commission into Children's Employment (Mines). © National Coal Mining Museum for England

Stage two

One of the major concerns of Lord Ashley was not simply the fact that women and girls were working underground, but the way they had to work closely with men who might be stripped bare. The eroding of the role of females as mothers and home-keepers in family life was seen as being of serious concern.

Ask the students to listen to a song, based on Patience's words. There are recent recordings of this song available.[6] Alternatively, reading the song out loud to the group will suffice. The students will need copies of the lyrics re-printed here.

Child labour

> **Testimony of Patience Kershaw (Frank Higgins)**
>
> It's good of you to ask me, Sir, to tell you how I spend my days.
> Down in a coal black tunnel, Sir, I hurry corves to earn my pay.
> The corves are full of coal, kind Sir, I push them with my hands and head.
> It isn't lady-like, but Sir, you've got to earn your daily bread.
>
> I push them with my hands and head, and so my hair gets worn away.
> You see this baldy patch I've got, it shames me like I just can't say.
> A lady's hands are lily white, but mine are full of cuts and segs.
> And since I'm pushing all the time, I've got great big muscles on my legs.
>
> I try to be respectable, but sir, the shame, God save my soul.
> I work with naked, sweating men who curse and swear and hew the coal.
> The sights, the sounds, the smells, kind Sir, not even God could know my pain.
> I say my prayers, but what's the use? Tomorrow will be just the same.
>
> Now, sometimes, Sir, I don't feel well, my stomach's sick, my head it aches.
> I've got to hurry best I can. My knees are weak, my back near breaks.
> And then I'm slow, and then I'm scared these naked men will batter me.
> But they're not to blame, for if I'm slow, their families will starve, you see.
>
> Now all the lads, they laugh at me, and Sir, the mirror tells me why.
> Pale and dirty can't look nice. It doesn't matter how hard I try.
> Great big muscles on my legs, a baldy patch upon my head.
> A lady, Sir? Oh, no, not me! I should've been a boy instead.
>
> I praise your good intentions, Sir, I love your kind and gentle heart.
> But now it's 1842, and you and I, we're miles apart.
> A hundred years and more will pass before we're standing side by side.
> But please accept my grateful thanks. God bless you Sir, at least you tried.

Play the song and hand out or project the lyrics, checking that everyone understands the northern dialect.

Divide the whole group into groups of four or five. Ask each group to take two verses of the song lyrics. Using only the words of the song, they are to create a series of still images or moving mime sequences that capture Patience's experience. Encourage the groups to think abstractly – how they might use their bodies to create the corves, tunnels, and other features of the mine, and the physically hard labour the miners endured.

Allow preparation time before sharing. If you have allocated verses of the song to each group, this can be done sequentially.

Perform each group's work in turn and evaluate the drama.

Protest songs

Over the years, popular music has given singers and composers the opportunity to write songs that protest about an issue, voice a political opinion or raise awareness about a moral or social wrong. Some of these songs are very direct and forceful in their lyrics, while others use metaphors and symbolism to make their point. Many of the songs become *anthems*, associated with certain movements.

There have been many songs that are anti-war in their sentiment. Singer songwriters like Bob Dylan, Pete Seeger and John Lennon have all contributed to this genre. John Lennon's *Give Peace A Chance* became one of the anthems of the Vietnam anti-war protest in the 1960s and 1970s.

The American Civil Rights movement inspired many artists to compose songs that spoke of their dreams for equality and a brighter future. Sam Cooke's 1964 release, *A Change is Gonna Come*, captures perfectly the sentiment of Black Americans struggling against prejudice. Modern artists today still find social and political inequality a rich theme to explore through music, as did the folk singers of the Industrial Revolution who sang of horrific working conditions, exploitation and poor pay.

Task: working in a small group of three or four, discuss why you think music might be a good way to get a message across to a large audience.

Do some research on music for change and protest songs: investigate the following very different artists and their music. What do you think the songs are about? Do you think they are effective in getting their message across? Which words or imagery in the lyrics are most effective, do you think?

- Bob Dylan – *Blowin' In the Wind*

- John Lennon – *Give Peace a Chance*

- U2 – *Sunday Bloody Sunday*

- The Clash – *Clampdown*

- Robert Wyatt (Elvis Costello) – *Ship Building*

- Billy Bragg (Pete Seeger) – *Which Side Are You On?*

- Marvin Gaye – *What's Going On / What's Happening Brother?*

- Joni Mitchell – *Big Yellow Taxi*

Are you aware of any contemporary artists writing and singing 'protest' songs?[7]

Stage three

Explain to the group that the final part of this section will explore two opposing sides of the reforming debate. Although Lord Ashley's commission was shocking to the general public, there was significant resistance to any sort of reform from the politicians who passed the laws. Why might that be?

Child labour

Divide the room into two areas and put equal numbers of students on both sides. Explain that one side of the room represents the attitude of the coal mine owners and politicians who see the child workers as necessary. The other side of the room will take on the roles of the reformers who want an end to children and women working underground. The reformers will have the chance to present their ideas first and try to convince the Members of Parliament to vote to create new laws designed to protect children.

It might be worth exploring some of the arguments and counter-arguments involved in this debate. First the reformers:

- Children and women are being exploited.
- The work is too dangerous for children and deaths and accidents are commonplace.
- Children should be kept away from the coarse behaviour and language of the adult miners.
- Children should be taught to read and write in organized schools.
- Children should not work such long hours, often alone and in darkness.
- Children should not be made to do such hard labour, which caused deformities and illnesses in their developing bodies.
- Laws have been made to protect children in factories and mills, why not mines?

Those against reform might say:

- Child labour keeps the price of coal down – removing them from the mines will make coal more expensive.
- A profitable pit is more likely to be kept open for the whole community to work in.
- The children's wages supplement the income of their family and families often work together as a team.
- The accepted norm is that all children work and hard work makes people proud and self-sufficient.
- If the children did not do these poorly paid jobs, then who *would* do them?
- There is no need to educate working class children – why do children need to go to school if they are destined for the factories or mines anyway?

Allow each group time to prepare their arguments. Tell them they will only have a few seconds to express their thoughts, so they need to be concise and focused. Once the groups are prepared, ask them to sit in their assigned space, opposite a group with the opposing view. Explain that each group will have a short time to present their ideas to you as *The Speaker*.

Allow time for a plenary evaluation:

- Who had the better argument?
- Which side made the argument most forcibly?
- Can the group understand why the historical debate proved difficult to resolve?

Creative writing

This exercise is a creative writing task that could be developed into a song or piece of music.

Writing from the point of view of people attempting to change the working conditions of the miners, and end the practice of children working underground in the pits, compose a poem that highlights some of the issues that have been discussed in the previous exercise.

Consider a repeated verse that identifies what the benefits of reform could be, and has a *call to action*, such as:

A child's life should be free from pain,

And a day's full work takes a terrible strain,

Learning and playing should be their right,

Let's take them all from darkness to light.

If you make sure that your poem has a simple structure, like *rhyming couplets*, then you will be able to set it to music more easily.

Remind yourself of the protest songs and songs for change discussed earlier; are there any structures you could copy or adapt? Consider composing your poem or song in the first person, as someone giving testimony similar to *The testimony of Patience Kershaw*. Alternatively, write your lyrics from the point of view of a witness, horrified at what they encountered down in the mines.

At a depth of one mile, the air is so thick,

And all can be heard is the strike of the pick,

The curses and cries of those all condemned,

To a childhood of toil at the coalface they tend.

This task can be completed individually or in a small group. Your poem or song can be performed or recorded.

Section four – child labour in the present day

Stage one

The final section of this work introduces the issue of modern child labour. There is a great deal of information freely available to teachers on the Internet that will allow you to illustrate your teaching with images, video and vivid accounts of the experience of young children in some parts of the world. UNICEF (Unicef.com) is a charity that is concerned with the plight of child workers and has some very useful information, accounts and links to explore.

As a starter activity, and to introduce the modern context of this section, ask the group to suggest the sort of part-time jobs children who are still attending school

Child labour

might undertake; examples might be paper rounds, babysitting or working in restaurants or shops.

Now explain that there are lots of rules about the sort of work young people and children can do. Present the current government rules relating to children and work:

> - A child is someone under the age of 14 and a young person is someone under the school leaving age of 16.
>
> - Young people under school leaving age (16) are only allowed to do light work. They cannot work in a factory or construction, in transport, in a mine or on a registered merchant ship.
>
> - Children under the age of 14 are not allowed to work at all. Unless it is to take part in sport, advertising, modelling, plays, films, television or other entertainment.
>
> - Children can do odd jobs for a parent, relative or neighbour.
>
> - Children can do babysitting.
>
> - Children who are 13 or above may be able to do jobs that are not considered to be a hazard to health, safety of development – such as delivering a paper round.

There are strict limits to the amount of time children and young people can work, which are designed to stop children taking time off school, and to ensure that they don't get too tired and have enough holidays.

Ask the group whether they think these rules are important.

Do they think that these rules apply all over the world?

In February 2010, UNICEF launched their five-year 'Put it Right' campaign, highlighting the abuse of children's rights around the world.[8]

The campaign features a startling video, widely available on the World Wide Web, which is filmed in a variety of countries and features the music of Radiohead. Prepare the group for the startling images they are about to see and share the video 'Put It Right?'[9]

After watching the video ask the group to consider the following question:

'If Patience Kershaw could visit the twenty-first century from the past, what would she think? Have things improved since her day?'

Stage two

Explain that for the next part of the work the students will develop a prepared improvisation based on the lives of working children in developing countries. Divide the class into working groups of four or five and tell them that they will base their work on the words of child labourers from different parts of the world. Hand out the extracts and allow time to discuss the implications of each account.

Write or project the word *narration*. 'If someone is a narrator in a play, what do they do?'

Explain that using a narrator can alter the relationship that the performers have with the dramatic action, and can also affect the way the audience relates to the performance, making it much 'cooler' and more objective.

This is often referred to as an *alienation* or 'distancing' effect and, following the work of *Bertolt Brecht*, is used in theatre to enable the audience to engage more with the content and ideas of the drama, rather than being a 'passive' spectator who is swept away with the story, simply content to watch the drama unfold.

The epic theatre of Bertolt Brecht

Bertolt Brecht (1898–1956) was a German poet, playwright and theatre director who developed an approach to theatre making that challenged the accepted notions of how an audience relates to the action and characters of conventional 'dramatic' theatre. His famous plays include *Mother Courage and Her Children, The Threepenny Opera* and *The Caucasian Chalk Circle,* and he wrote extensively about his theoretical ideas for transforming the stage. He is one of the most influential theatre practitioners of the twentieth century, and alongside Stanislavski is a towering figure in the history of modernist theatre.

Brecht's theatre was explicitly political and he wanted his audience to maintain their ability to think objectively and make decisions about the content of his plays, without being bogged down in a *cathartic* or overtly emotional response to what they saw on stage. To facilitate this, Brecht introduced a number of techniques into his productions that were designed to remind the audience that they were watching a play being performed by actors. The audience could still feel emotionally involved in the play, but their emotional involvement was supposed to prompt action and indignation, rather than acceptance and empathy. He wanted his audience to feel contrary emotions to the characters on stage.

One of the key concepts of Brecht's aesthetic was termed 'verfremdungseffekt'; often translated as 'to make strange'. He made the theatre experience unfamiliar and unsettling for his audiences by using direct address spoken straight to the audience, titles and placards that indicated what would happen at the start of scenes, music and song in the action, narration, flashback, and a style of acting where the emphasis is upon actors to 'demonstrate' their characters rather than 'become' their roles on stage. By doing this, he hoped audiences would maintain a sense of distance from the emotional content of the play and focus upon the political injustices and moral compromises being portrayed.

Brecht worked in collaboration with other artists throughout his life, and he worked with musicians such as Kurt Weill and theatre designers such as Caspar Neher to create startling productions that marked out the highly stylized form that became known as *Epic Theatre*.

Brecht was very much a product of his time, a committed Marxist and promoter of socialist issues, he spent some of his life living in exile in America after fleeing the Nazis of Hitler's Germany. Once the war was over, he left America after testifying in front of the *House Committee on Un-American Activities* who were convinced he was a communist. Brecht finally returned to Europe – to East Berlin, where he died of a heart attack aged 58.

Child labour

There are many different ways of incorporating a narrator into the drama. Here are a few suggestions:

- The narration is presented as a *voiceover* and is spoken in the first or third person. The narrator stands to one side, the rear or the front of the stage as the action is presented and is not acknowledged by the actors.

- A *storyteller*, who controls the action – often by commenting on, moving or freezing the actors on stage – speaks the narration in the first or third person.

- The narration is again spoken in the first or third person, but by the actors themselves, with each performer 'stepping out' of the action to directly address the audience and describe what they are doing.

Explain that for this task, groups will need to use the words of the extracts as narration, and must develop appropriate dramatic action to 'illustrate' the text.

This action could be interpreted in an abstract manner by being broken down into a series of still images, slow motion gestures or mime, or repeated phrases (*motifs*) of movement performed in unison or in canon. Other groups might prefer to focus on a more naturalistic approach, still incorporating narration, but trying to be as realistic as possible in their portrayal of the child labourer's tasks.

Allow sufficient time for the groups to prepare their work. Work should be performed where possible without scripts, the emphasis being on the emotive content of the drama rather than the accuracy of the spoken text.

Child labour in the present day resource sheet

It is estimated that 218 million children worldwide are involved in child labour of some sort. Children can carry out a range of different jobs in many different categories from brick making, mining, domestic work, through to stitching footballs and weaving rugs.

Not all child work is classed as child labour. Part-time jobs that are safe, legal and do not impact negatively upon a child's life can be a positive experience.

Halima's story: Bangladesh

*My name is **Halima** and I am 11 years old. I work in a clothing factory in Bangladesh. My job is to trim off the loose threads from the shorts once they have been machined. The scissors are sharp and heavy. We all sit in rows and as soon as I have finished one pile of clothes, another pile arrives. I work for around 12 hours a day, but the day can be longer if there is a large order that needs to be finished. It's harder at night because the light in the factory isn't bright enough to see. I do not have any time to go to school or see my family, my life revolves around the factory.*

When I get tired and slow down, my employer hits or slaps me. He calls me lazy and makes me work faster. Although I work all day, I'm not paid any money because my mother borrowed money from the factory owner, so now I work to pay back my family's debt but the debt never seems to get less.

Amitosh's story[10]: India

***Amitosh** is 10 years old. He works for up to 16 hours a day sewing plastic beads onto children's clothes by hand.*

'I was bought from my parents' village in [the northern state of] Bihar and taken to New Delhi by train,' he says. 'The men came looking for us in July. They had loudspeakers in the back of a car and told my parents that, if they sent me to work in the city, they won't have to work in the farms. My father was paid a fee for me and I was brought down with 40 other children. The journey took 30 hours and we weren't fed. I've been told I have to work off the fee the owner paid for me so I can go home, but I am working for free. I am a shaagird [a pupil]. The supervisor has told me because I am learning I don't get paid. It has been like this for four months.'

Chou's story: Cambodia

I work on the city rubbish dump. I started when I was six years old and now I am eight. We get up before dawn and use lights on our heads so we can see. We look for plastic bottles, scraps of paper or anything metal.

I carry a big sack on my shoulder and have a long metal hook with a wooden handle which I use to scrape the ground. Sometimes you've got to dig into the rubbish piles to find the best things. Once your bag is full, you take it to the men who give you money for it.

Sometimes I get sick from being on the dump, because people from the city put anything into their trash and it ends up here. When the smell gets too bad, we light fires to burn the rubbish, but the smoke can make your eyes water, so I tie a scarf around my face. You have to be careful not to get crushed by the trucks that bring the rubbish in from the city. There is always a rush to be first when they tip out a new load. The drivers don't see us when they reverse, they are always in a hurry. It is easy to get caught under the wheels.

Child labour

When the groups are ready, explain that they will be sharing their performances with a character they have met before. You will again be taking on the role of Patience Kershaw, 'visiting' from the past, who will be able to comment on how much has changed since her testimony in 1842. (Alternatively, this role could be assigned to a confident student, who, at the end of each presentation, could be asked for their opinion as Patience.)

Start the sequence of performances and at the end of each one, as Patience, comment upon the drama.

I thought that things might have changed.

I see myself, and my kin, in these children.

Their lives are just like ours were back in the year 1842.

It's a disgrace that in your so-called modern world, so many children are robbed of their childhood.

What have the politicians done? Where are the laws to protect these children?

Once all the work has been shared, encourage the students to reflect on what they have learnt so far. Remind them that millions of children are full-time workers worldwide. Many of the jobs they do are dangerous, unregulated and poorly paid – or even not paid at all.

Poverty is recognized as being a root cause of child labour. Ask the students if they think this is acceptable in a modern world? What is the solution? What should countries and their governments do to help protect their children?

Stage three

In pairs, ask the students to decide on a single law they would pass, if they had the power to do so, that would stop the exploitation of working children. After a few minutes share their responses. Are there any common ideas? Is there a single solution to the problem? Should the same rules apply in all cases?

Because the issues around child labour are emotive and challenging, charities such as *Save the Children* are careful not to generalize on these matters, believing that to do so might lead people to draw conclusions that are misleading or counter-productive. Their approach to addressing issues around child labour is one of supporting the rights of each child in his or her specific situation:

We believe that children's work is not a uniform activity and we must recognise that, while some forms of work violate children's development and well being, other types of work activities do not.

We accept neither blanket bans of all child work, nor an approach that promotes children's work in general. We believe that different responses are appropriate for different forms of work and different working children.

All our work is based on a rights-based approach. Rights are interdependent and what affects one right will usually affect others. This holistic view of rights means it is crucial to gain a full understanding of the links between children's rights and the relationship between them, for example the right to be free from harmful work alongside other rights, such as the right to survival.

Source: http://www.savethechildren.org.uk/eyetoeye/childlabour/ourapproach.htm

Save the Children's experience has shown that a blanket ban on employing children in some countries and cultures might not work. Some of the reasons for failure are listed below:

- There may be a strong ethical and cultural precedent for children to work.
- Work can help support a child's right to survival, paying for food, clothes, shelter and possibly education.
- Work can help develop important skills that may be useful in life.
- Work can develop self-esteem and the feeling that the child is contributing to the family. This contribution can give them the opportunity to participate in the decisions of the family.

Likewise, ignoring the exploitation of children in the workplace is wrong for the following reasons:

- A working life does not combine well with going to school and children are losing the right to an education; poor education traps children in a cycle of low-skilled work.
- Some work denies children the right to protection; children can be mistreated by their employers; some work will put children in conflict with the police where they risk arrest.
- Some work is dangerous or hazardous and can have a negative effect upon their physical well-being.

Child labour

- Some work can have a very harmful physical effect: in the worst cases it can kill.

Stage four

For the concluding exercise, begin by reading out the following petition from Bangladeshi child workers:

Our fellow young workers who were terminated from the garments industry have either become child prostitutes or brick breakers or garbage collectors . . . we appeal to allow us to continue our light work for 5–6 hours a day and give us an opportunity to attend school for 2–3 hours a day. If you find child workers in any hazardous or heavy work, bring them back to light work. Do not throw away on the streets those of us who are already involved in some kind of light work.[11]

Ask the students to return to their previous groups from the narration task. Provide large sheets of paper and pens and explain the following;

Thinking about your previous drama: write a list of three strategies that might work to support the children from your particular account. Now, frame these as 'rights' or demands. These might be things like;

- *The right to light work that does not have a negative effect upon health and well-being.*
- *The right to short working days.*
- *The right to regular breaks, food and refreshment.*
- *The right to fair pay.*
- *The right to attend school and be educated.*
- *The right to work safely in a safe environment.*
- *The right to be treated fairly without the threat of violence or intimidation.*
- *The right not to be involved in bonded labour or labour based around paying back a family debt.*

Once all the groups are happy with their list of 'rights', inform them that they are going to present these demands within a short piece of theatre. To provide a frame for the work, explain that the audience for this drama will be a panel of government ministers. The students will be working as a small group of actors creating a piece of *Agitprop* theatre.

Agitprop Theatre – from *agitation* and *propaganda* – directly addresses social or political issues and attempts to provoke a response for change in its audience. It originated in the former USSR in the 1920s as a means of communicating political messages to a largely illiterate population. Recognizable by its use of physical style, stock characters and direct leftist politics, the Agitprop *Blue Blouse* movement spread to other countries in Europe, notably Weimar Germany, where it directly influenced the theatre of the young Bertolt Brecht. Agitprop also appeared in the UK alternative theatre scene of the 1970s and 1980s when Marxist theatre companies such as Leeds' *Red Ladder* (which celebrated its 40th birthday in 2008[12]) and CAST (*Cartoon Archetypal Slogan Theatre*) took up the form. *Red Ladder* was named after the archetypal agitprop stage piece; a ladder could instantly represent the social hierarchy – capitalists at the top and workers below, providing an accessible metaphor for revolutionary change. It would also fit in the back of a van and could become a portable platform for street theatre or other impromptu performances.

The students' drama will attempt to convince the panel of the need to identify strategies and initiate projects that recognize the rights of children.

Their starting point is their previous work, which they should adapt to include the list of rights they have devised. These could be presented in the form of spoken captions or titles, inserted at different points in the drama. The pieces could include illustrations of what might happen to working children without such rights being granted, and groups should be encouraged to find a quick, physical, accessible style.

There are a number of techniques which could be employed to create appropriately hard-hitting effects: one possibility is to encourage students to experiment with a *lip-syncing* technique by having the language of the 'demand' spoken by one or more members of the group as another character mouths the words. This technique can create an unsettling and disjointed theatrical effect that highlights the shared experience of the child workers – literally, many voices in one body.

Allow enough time for the groups to prepare their presentations, before identifying a performance area. Remind the groups that, as audience members, they are receiving the work as a panel of politicians who have the power to pass laws and instigate change.

Share the work:

How effective were the *agitprop* pieces?

How far has the project as a whole raised awareness of issues relating to child labour?

Is it realistic to expect drama to influence social change? Could the group research examples where theatre – or television drama – has altered the way that people think about particular issues?

The resources for this Unit are available for download at www.routledge.com/9780415572064

The Phaeton Project

Figure 5.1 Depicted on an Ancient Greek bowl, Helios, the sun god, drives his chariot of fire through the heavens

Thematic content in this unit:	Curriculum connections:
Greek myths	English, History
Ancient cosmology	Science
Origin stories and legends	English, RE
Metaphors and analogies	English

Dramatic techniques and keywords in this unit:

Parallel play	Chamber Theatre	Hubris	Eyewitness accounts
Nemesis	Analogy	Unison	Soundscape
Cross-cutting	Marking the moment		

In this unit students will explore a classic Greek myth – the story of Phaeton – using drama as a medium to draw connections between the original story and contemporary ecological concerns.

They are first framed as reporters working for a newspaper who are asked to look to the Greek myth in order to make sense of a modern-day mystery. In their explorations they have opportunities to dramatize the Phaeton story, and then to draw upon their understandings to trace contemporary parallels or analogies.

Where this unit connects

This unit provides opportunities for learning across a number of curriculum areas. The unit starts by establishing a contemporary context based around a potential ecological disaster, which arises when a top-secret project goes wrong. As such, the drama will resonate with a number of 'recent' events – perhaps most obviously the huge Gulf of Mexico oil spill of autumn 2010 – and will ask students to consider the moral and ethical implications of mankind's exploitation of the Earth for wealth and resources. The focus of the work switches as students, working in role as newspaper reporters, have to examine a classic Greek myth, in which a headstrong young man challenges his father's authority, over-reaches himself and ultimately brings disaster on himself – and almost destroys the Earth in the process. The original drama frame – that of print journalists researching a story – should motivate students to want to explore the myth for the light it might shed on the contemporary puzzle they need to solve. In terms of the curriculum the unit will therefore extend to work on Greek myths, beliefs and society, the moral responsibility of the scientist and ecological issues – global warming, soil erosion, etc. The unit will engage students in a range of drama techniques including chamber theatre, figurative mime and so on, as a means of active exploration of the key concepts of *hubris* and *nemesis* within a story which still speaks to us across the centuries.

Working in drama: by the end of this unit students will have:

- Worked in role as print journalists researching a 'whistle-blower's' revelations.
- Explored a Greek myth using an 'eyewitness' account on which to base soundscapes aiming to create atmosphere, mood and tension.
- Used the technique of *chamber theatre* to dramatize the story.
- Devised their own contemporary analogies or parallels to the Greek myth, using a structured approach.

The Phaeton Project

Section one

Stage one – the newsroom

The class is presented with the following:

PHAETON PROJECT GOES CRITICAL

Earth in peril as a result of 'arrogant' director, claims scientist

"... I warned him, but he didn't listen"

Dr James Jones, the scientist caught up in the recent scandal over the top-secret Phaeton Project, has today warned the government that the power unleashed by the experimental energy source could 'melt the Earth'. "The thing is out of control", he commented, "and could go critical at any time ... this project has to be stopped. Someone has to listen to reason before it is too late. They don't know what they've unleashed – but it could destroy life on Earth and leave our planet a barren wilderness."

Greet the students as Jo(e) Willis, Editor of *The Weekly Report*, a national newspaper:

Right – is all the News Team assembled? Good – time is short. I want you to look at this mock-up of next week's edition. We're ready to run with this – it could be the biggest story of the century! We have an exclusive lead from this Dr Jones. Apparently he used to be a senior scientist on the Phaeton Project, but he suddenly resigned. The day after, I received a phone call where he started to give me the story, but then we got cut off. I want to go with the story; the only problem is we need to check some detail. We can't publish until we're absolutely sure of the facts. That's where you come in ... I want you to do a bit of investigating. Find out about this Dr Jones – and the Phaeton Project – find out what it is, who's in charge and what's gone wrong ... now, get into your working teams and come up with a plan of action ...

Out of role, ask the students to reflect on the drama so far: check their understanding of the situation and their role, and the task that has been assigned. Lead them back into the task by asking them to plan their investigation – *we need to interview this Dr Jones – what do we need to ask him?*

Ask each group to record two or three questions for Dr Jones, which, in role as the Editor you can check and 'choreograph': ... *that's a great question; when Dr Jones arrives, you can ask the first question ...*

Take on the role of Dr Jones, using a role signifier such as a hat or overcoat to help differentiate the role from the previous one of Editor of *The Weekly Record*.

Dr Jones is nervous, and quite evasive when asked direct questions: *I have agreed to meet with you ... but I can't stay long ...*

Dr Jones signals to the class that he can't say much – he's afraid – even fears for his life. He does, though, make reference to someone known as 'P', who is 'an upstart – out of control'. He tells them:

- The Phaeton Project is highly secret – *security priority one.*

- The project is to set up an experimental energy source aimed at harnessing the power of sunlight with the potential to provide enough clean energy for all time.

- Things were going well on the project until the mysterious 'P', *forced us to take things too far . . . that's when I resigned . . . but I think we may already be too late . . .*

I can't say anything else – but I warn you – you have to stop him! The clue is in the name of the project! You must understand . . . I am so ashamed! 'P' is my son!

Out of role, ask the students to reflect on Dr Jones' final warning:

What could he mean, 'the clue is in the name'?

Finish the first teaching session on this 'cliffhanger!'

In order to continue our investigation we will need to go back in time – to another place and another world . . . to investigate the story of Phaeton!

Section two – the amber tears: the myth of Phaeton

Stage one – an eyewitness account

Project the image of Helios driving his chariot through the heavens.

In pairs, ask the students to share their thoughts about the image.

- Who might the person in the image be?

- What is he doing?

Share the students' ideas.

Give some of the context of the image, and explain the link between Helios and Phaeton. Explain that the class will need to investigate the story of Phaeton before they will be able to understand Dr Jones' warning!

Distribute the following account to the class: *To start our investigation of the story of Phaeton we have an eyewitness account of events right at the end of the tale.*

Project the eyewitness account, so that the class can follow as you read through. Ask them to take special note of any sounds described in the piece, as they are going to help enhance the atmosphere of a second reading using the technique of *sound-scape.* Take suggestions, and allow groups of students time to compose short sections of soundscape. Read the text a second time, allowing space for students to add what they have composed.

The Phaeton Project

An eyewitness account

Let me recount what I have witnessed: my comrades and I were on a great journey that had caused us to travel over half the world. Exhausted by our quest for the Golden Fleece, we were glad to finally turn for home. On our return we entered the waters of the great river Eridanus and sailed as far as ships can go, into a great lake that opened out before us. It got hotter and hotter . . . we were engulfed in clouds of steam and smoke so that we were unable to see our hands in front of our faces. By day we were plagued by the nauseating stench of burning flesh; by night we were unable to sleep because of an eerie wailing that chilled our hearts. We slowly drew nearer and the sound grew louder and more shrill. We became aware of golden droplets in the water of the lake – they shone like the sun. Some of our sailors tried to grab them . . . but their hands were burned in the scalding water.

Finally we came upon a tomb with a carved inscription. Tall poplar trees surrounded the tomb; the trees were screaming and moaning! It was not until we drew near that we saw that the trees had women's faces and human arms and hands. Their eyes wept golden tears of amber, dried by the sun upon the sand; whenever the water of the lake lapped at the shore the amber tears were swept into the river.

They gestured to us 'Who approaches the daughters of Helios as they lament for their brother . . .?'

Who can help me make sense of what I have seen?

Stage two – the investigation

Out of role, ask the students to reflect on the episode:

- Where is the action taking place?
- What do they think is going on?
- Who is the traveller recounting the story?
- What might be the connection between the traveller, the story and the image?
- What of the references to heat – steam, smoke, burning flesh?
- Who is the figure in the image?
- What of the women transformed into trees?
- Who is their 'brother'?

In small groups ask the students to consider their responses to these prompts; share findings.

Section three – the story of Phaeton: hubris and Nemesis

> **Hubris**: extreme haughtiness or arrogance. Hubris often indicates a loss of touch with reality and overestimating one's own competence or capabilities.
>
> In many cases, people overcome by hubris will bring about their own downfall.
>
> **Nemesis**: the punisher of hubris; the goddess of divine indignation and retribution, who punished excessive pride, evil deeds, undeserved happiness or good fortune, and the absence of moderation.

Stage one

Explain that in order to continue their investigation the class will have to piece together the ancient story from ten episodes:

1

In ancient Ethiopia there lived a young man by the name of Phaeton. Although Phaeton was a mortal, his father was the sun god, Helios, himself.

One day, Phaeton was boasting to his friends that he was the son of mighty Helios. His friends taunted him, saying that he and his mother had made up the story.

Phaeton told his mother, and asked her to prove that he really was Helios' son. His mother told Phaeton that if he needed proof he could travel far to the east, where Helios had a golden palace.

2

Phaeton was excited by the idea and prepared himself for the long and dangerous journey to the east. He travelled through strange lands until he finally came to the high mountains that marked the eastern end of the world.

The boy climbed higher and higher, and soon came to a gigantic palace of gold and bronze. Massive silver doors marked the entrance. On them were strange carvings of gods and depictions of the world of mortals.

3

Phaeton walked through the silver doors and was dazzled by what he saw. There sat Helios, dressed in purple robes, sitting on a huge throne of precious emeralds. Many attendants surrounded him. When he spoke, Phaeton found it hard to look at Helios, so dazzling was the light that radiated from him.

4

Helios spoke:
Why do you come here, to the farthest corner of the Earth, Phaeton?

Phaeton replied that he had come to find proof that Helios was his father.

The sun god answered: *Your mother spoke the truth: I am your father. As proof, I swear that I will grant you one wish. I will grant anything your heart may desire.*

Without thinking, Phaeton demanded that he be allowed to drive his father's chariot across the heavens. Helios immediately regretted his promise, and tried to dissuade the boy, saying that this was too dangerous a request for a mortal boy to undertake.

5

But Phaeton had his mind set on driving the chariot of the sun god, and Helios could not break his oath. With a heavy heart, his father agreed. The attendants coupled the impatient horses to the chariot, and Aurora, goddess of dawn, opened the palace curtains to fill the sky with the first light of day. *It is time. My son, will you not re-consider? Even now, it is not too late . . . Let me take your place?*

But Phaeton was a determined youth and he insisted that his father should not disappoint him.

Phaeton climbed into the chariot and Helios placed the crown of the sun on his son's head.

6

Phaeton could feel the mighty horses straining at their leash, snorting fire and scraping sparks with their hooves . . . and then they were off, galloping away with poor Phaeton left struggling to contain their power and fury.

They immediately tried to ride higher than Phaeton knew they should, but he did not have the strength to stop them. The Earth became smaller and more distant with each minute that passed. Soon all of the earth was in total darkness.

Phaeton gave one last heave against the reins, but the furious horses surged with such power that he dropped the reins completely. The chariot suddenly changed direction and careered back towards the frozen, dark planet below.

7

As the chariot came nearer to the Earth, the temperature rose rapidly. Mighty rivers dried up. Forests, parched dry, erupted in flames. Cities burned. The chariot charged across the heavens, leaving destruction in its wake. Mighty forests were burned to dust; large parts of northern Africa and Asia were reduced to nothing but desert.

8

Zeus viewed the events with horror. Afraid that the whole world would be destroyed, he hurled a huge thunderbolt at the chariot. The lightning smashed the chariot and it crashed to Earth, a gigantic ball of flames and smoke. Phaeton was killed outright and came to land in the river Eridanos, in modern day Italy.

9

Phaeton's three sisters were stricken with grief and wept for him in the place where he perished.

They built for him a stone tomb, marked with an inscription. Zeus eventually took pity on them and turned them into poplar trees. Their tears, where they fell into the river, became golden amber.

According to some scholars these events were witnessed by the Argonauts in their travels to find The Golden Fleece.

10

Vulcan, the blacksmith of the gods, quickly repaired the chariot, but Helios, mourning for his dead son, refused to drive it. The next day the Earth remained dark and cold. Eventually Zeus persuaded Helios, and the following day he again drove the fiery chariot in its correct course across the heavens.

Divide the group into sub-groups, and give each group one or two sections of the story.

Ask each group to read their section, and dramatize it as 'chamber theatre' – without using dialogue, but using the text as narrative. Everything referred to in the passage must be represented on stage, the text must be spoken as written. Encourage the creative solving of 'technical' problems (such as the chariot flying, world burning, etc.!) *What techniques could we use to depict these 'difficult' episodes of the story?*

Some suggestions: narration; choral speaking; depictions (tableaux); placards; drawings; paper 'labels', simple puppets, paper costumes, figurative mime, physical theatre.

> **Chamber theatre** is a useful technique in adapting literary texts for performance. The aim is to retain as much as possible of the work's original text. Narration as well as dialogue can be included, often performed by multiple actors, as in David Edgar's celebrated adaptation of Dickens' *The Life and Adventures of Nicholas Nickleby*, in which characters provide their own third person narrative. Staging of chamber theatre pieces is usually minimal, with scenic units brought in and out in view of the audience, or created by the actors themselves using figurative mime.

Stage two

Once prepared, enact the sections in chronological order so that all students become familiar with the story.

Can they now answer the questions set by the mysterious eyewitness account? Go back to the initial questions and fill in as many gaps as possible.

Ask the students to reflect on the story: what is the story 'about'?

Can they begin to understand Dr Jones' strange warning? Why would he want them to investigate the Greek myth in order to understand what had gone wrong with the contemporary 'Phaeton Project'?

Section four

One theory about the function of myths in the ancient Greek world is that they conveyed explanations of the mysteries of creation, of natural phenomena, and mankind's relationship with the world. In this tradition, within this single story can be found a cosmological explanation of the movement of the heavens and the existence of night and day, as well as the origins of African deserts, amber, and the Milky Way!

So, on one level, whilst the story deals with perhaps familiar themes: a father with great power is contrasted with a son keen to prove himself; an oath is taken which cannot be kept; at a moment of reckless abandon a young man experiences 'god-like' feelings before facing his 'nemesis', on another, it also gives us clues to the ways in which people in the ancient world might have thought about the world and their place within it.

In the case of the story of Phaeton, and other similar myths such as the story of *Icarus*, there are clear references to the dangers of youthful *hubris*. With Phaeton, however, it is not just personal injury and humiliation that is the consequence of his recklessness, but cataclysmic events, which threaten the whole Earth and everyone on it.

In this section we are hoping to draw connections between this myth of the ancient world and contemporary concerns by asking the students to trace a contemporary parallel, or analogy, to the original story.

Analogies suggest similar relationships between different things (A is to B as C is to D)

An example from theatre is in Brecht's *Caucasian Chalk Circle* where a dispute between peasant farmers over who has the right to cultivate a fertile valley is presented as an analogy to a dispute over a child between its legal mother, who abandoned it, and the woman who has cared for it.

In drama, analogies work because they can allow audiences to see something from another perspective, or introduce complexity and depth through reference to something that the audience already grasps or understands.

Stage one

Start by asking the students the following questions, aiming to tease out links between the Phaeton story and contemporary contexts:

- *Can anyone see any similarities between the story of Phaeton and things happening today?*
- *In looking for parallels between the myth and the present day, who might Phaeton be, or represent? Who or what could Helios be?*
- *What is a contemporary equivalent of Helios' chariot?*

- *What might the threat to the world represented in the story become in today's world?*

- *How might this help us to understand Dr Jones' warning? How far could the Phaeton Project story be an analogy for the ancient myth?*

Stage two

Table 5.1 Phaeton and modern parallels

NAME/ OBJECT	MODERN PARALLEL?	REPRESENTING WHAT?	TO WHAT END?
Phaeton	Mankind/the director of the 'Phaeton Project'	Unrelenting need for more power	The earth is threatened with extinction by global warming.
Helios	The government	Control and regulation	Loses the argument, ending in disaster
Helios' chariot	Nuclear power	Unlimited power – at a price.	Could go either way – depending on how humans use it

Create groups of four and give each group a table on which to record their thinking.

Once they have a basic idea, explain to them that they are going to create a short presentation to the rest of the class (again in role as reporters) speculating as to what might have gone wrong in the top-secret Phaeton Project: the best ideas will become a short piece of documentary for the *Weekly Report* website. Ask them to pinpoint the precise moment when 'P' challenged his father's power to run the project effectively; how, precisely, did this happen?

Stage three

Present the groups' work. Evaluate:

- *Which of the ideas we saw worked best as parallels – or analogies – of the original Phaeton story?*

- *Why was the analogy successful?*

- *How could we tell the story of the Phaeton Project and why it went wrong by referring to the myth?*

- *Can we switch between modern-day scenes (perhaps showing the young, headstrong 'P' becoming more and more arrogant and determined) and the myth (showing Phaeton arguing with his father)?*

- *In the modern version, how might the story end? How might the world be 'saved'?*

Some suggested techniques:

- *Parallel play* – where two scenes, taking place at different times and places are established on stage at the same time, allowing for the action of the drama to move swiftly from one to the other, using the technique of . . .

- *Cross-cutting* – where, at a pre-arranged cue, the action of the drama moves from one scene to the next – usually through cross-fading stage lighting, or through the use of tableaux. This allows highly effective contrasts or juxtapositions to be created and lends the drama a degree of stylization.

- *Marking the moment* – where students select a significant moment in the drama to highlight, using a range of techniques: tableau, slow-motion, the use of narration, spoken thoughts or music.

Allow time for groups to map out their pieces along the following structure:

1 Contemporary scene showing the beginnings of the Phaeton Project and introducing the ambitious young scientist, 'P'.
2 A scene from the myth paralleling the first.
3 A scene that shows 'P's' *hubris* – the way he over-reaches himself in his desire for power.
4 A scene from the myth showing the same thing, leading to the fall of Phaeton.
5 A devised parallel scene showing what happens: how the world narrowly escapes disaster – and what happens to 'P'.

Perform and share reflections on the work.

Greek myths and legends

There are many other Greek myths that might also be seen as analogous with contemporary concerns.

In fact, some of them have become part of the way that we think about the world and have entered the language as commonplace metaphors.

Task: what is meant when something or someone is described as:

- *A Pandora's Box?*
- *Narcissistic?*
- *Flying too close to the sun?*
- *Having a Midas touch?*
- *A Trojan Horse?*
- *A Siren?*
- *A Gorgon?*

Can you research the original story which gave rise to the metaphor?

The resources for this Unit are available for download at www.routledge.com/9780415572064

Eyam plague village

Thematic content in this unit:	Curriculum connections:
An introduction to London's Great Plague of 1665	History
The history of Eyam, Derbyshire	History, Geography
Community and responsibility	Citizenship, PSHE
Epidemics and plagues	Science, Media Studies

Dramatic techniques and keywords in this unit:

The use of visual stimulus/pretext   Depiction

Dramatic reconstruction based on historical and fictional accounts

Parallel Play	Montage	Split stage and cross cutting
Whole group improvisation	Teacher in role	Defining the space
Tableaux and tableaux vivants	Caption making	Step out
Thought tracking	Narration	Atmosphere and dramatic tension
Spontaneous improvisation		

In this unit, students begin their drama by exploring events that happened in London during the Great Plague before the focus shifts towards a small Derbyshire village called Eyam (pronounced E'em). The year is 1665 and both communities are visited by the worst outbreak of plague since the Black Death of the 1300s.

What makes this story remarkable is the decision of the Eyam villagers to sacrifice themselves by not leaving the village boundary once the disease had established itself. In doing so, they spared their neighbours from the plague.

Tradition has it that the disease arrived in Eyam from London in a trunk of cloth ordered by the village tailor. In late August 1665 the trunk was delivered to the house

Eyam plague village

Alexander Hadfield shared with his wife Mary, two sons and hired hand George Viccars.

It was the unfortunate assistant George Viccars who opened the package and discovered that the rolls of cloth inside had become wet on their journey north from the capital. George realized he needed to act quickly and dry the damp cloth before it became spoiled further. Unrolling the damp material and laying it out to dry in front of the fire in the kitchen seemed to be the best thing to do.

It is assumed that this simple act allowed infected fleas carrying the plague that had been unwittingly transported in the cloth, to escape. In the absence of their usual host, the black rat, to feed on, the fleas turned to a human victim. On 7 September 1665 George Viccars became the first fatality of the plague in Eyam. Five more people died within three weeks, each of them close neighbours. Over the next nine months, a further 76 villagers perished.

It was in the summer of 1666 that William Mompesson, the rector of Eyam, along with his non-conformist predecessor Thomas Stanley, decided radical action needed to be taken to protect the villagers and their neighbours. Mompesson closed the church and suggested that families must bury their dead on their own land or in nearby fields. Church services would be held outside, to avoid people gathering together.

The most significant part of the plan, however, was to draw a *cordon sanitaire* around the whole village; a boundary that was not to be crossed by villagers or visitors. In effect, the surviving people of Eyam elected to cut themselves off from the rest of the world and try to contain the disease. This self-imposed quarantine relied upon the villagers promising not to leave at the time when they must have been most terrified.

Their resolve must have been sorely tested through the warm summer and autumn of 1666. These months saw the most deaths as the plague visited house after house. Whole families perished within days of each other, but still the villagers kept their promise not to leave. The final victim died on 1 November 1666. The plague had lasted 14 months and killed 260 people.

Where this unit connects

This unit explores a specific historical context, a time when a particular community made a tremendous sacrifice to prevent others coming to harm. As such, within **history** and **geography** it connects with other communities – and individuals – that have responded altruistically when in grave danger themselves. Examples might be drawn from recent events such as earthquakes and other natural disasters or more personal accounts of people who have sacrificed themselves to enable others to live.

It also connects with **science** through accounts of epidemics and pandemics, from *the Black Death* to *swine flu*, and the way in which communities, and in the latter case, the **media** respond to the idea of a *plague*.

> **Working in drama: by the end of this unit students will have:**
>
> - Worked in role with a teacher in an extended improvised drama.
>
> - Dramatized a seventeenth-century text using a range of drama techniques to create a dramatic *montage*.
>
> - Devised short pieces based around anecdotes and stories.
>
> - Created a dramatic commemoration to the people of Eyam as a means of reflection on the project.

Section one – London

Stage one

Explain to the students that our drama is to start in London. The year is 1665 and King Charles II is on the throne. It is July and the country is already experiencing an exceptionally hot summer.

Ask the students to form a large circle facing inwards. Explain that you will be taking on a role and miming an activity. Using the letter as a script, enact Charles Johnson, a fictional character who is a London merchant, packing up a parcel of cloth for dispatch to the North of England.

Dear Sir,

Please find within the following items as detailed in your earlier correspondence, to whit:

One roll of plain cotton
2 rolls of fine taffeta one of plain and one of emerald green
One roll of rose fine weave silk
One roll of the same – yellow
2 rolls of plum velvet

Assorted ribbons and lace and twist as described and required.

It is our hope Sir, that this package finds you in good health and in fine spirits. As you will know London is gripped by a severe contagion and we seem surrounded on all sides by plague pits and pest houses. Each week the Bills of Mortality are posted and each week the death count rises. Those that can have fled the city walls for fear of being shut in and, as such, this will be the last consignment of cloth I will be able to dispatch until the winter.

Nevertheless, the items you have ordered will surely serve you well in your task and allow the ladies and gentlemen of Derbyshire to dress in the latest and finest London fashions.

Eyam plague village

Your servant as ever,

Charles Johnson – Clothiers and merchants, Drury Lane, London

August 3rd 1665

Handing the mimed package to one of the students, finish by saying;

Make haste, and take this to the coaching station. They are expecting you. To be sent to Hadfield's the Tailors, Eyam village, Derbyshire, and make sure they take pains to pack the case carefully; it is a long journey.

Take a few moments to discuss the 'scene' and the spoken narrative. What do the students think might be the 'contagion' that has been mentioned? What do they know of the pest houses, plague pits and the Bills of Mortality that are mentioned? The merchant mentions people being 'shut in', what might this practice be referring to?

- *Pest houses* or huts were buildings used to house those dying of the plague.
- *Plague pits* were large mass graves dug to cater for the hundreds of deaths occurring daily.
- The *Bills of Mortality* were weekly printed records that were put up around the city detailing the numbers of dead and the parishes affected.
- *Shutting in* was the practice of confining victims to their dwellings, often with their healthy family.

Sum up the discussion by telling the students that our drama starts in London during the Great Plague of 1665. Explain that one of the most frightening things for the people of the time was that no-one really knew what caused the disease. There was plenty of evidence of what happened when people became ill but as for the reasons of *why* they became ill, the population was ignorant.

Stage two

The European Enlightenment and the Scientific Revolution of the seventeenth century were forging new ways of thinking and ways of making sense of the world. Observation and reason were becoming the principles of scientific endeavour but by modern standards the misunderstandings surrounding science and medicine can be challenging for students to grasp. To illustrate this, ask the students to get into pairs and label each other A and B and give the following instructions;

As, you have to explain to the Bs a difficult scientific phenomenon. The object of the exercise is to come up with your own convincing theory to explain the observed behaviour. It can be as far-fetched and imaginative as you like, but it must attempt to explain your hypothesis.

A magnetic object will attract certain metals; explain to your partner your ideas of how this works.

Allow a minute for the pairs to work together before sharing one or two of the more imaginative theories. Then repeat the exercise, this time with 'B' explaining to 'A' *why the sky is blue*. Were there any plausible explanations given?

Did anyone use religious or supernatural explanations to justify their theories?

Now create six groups of students and hand out the Great Plague resource sheet.

The Great Plague of London, 1665–1666 resource sheet

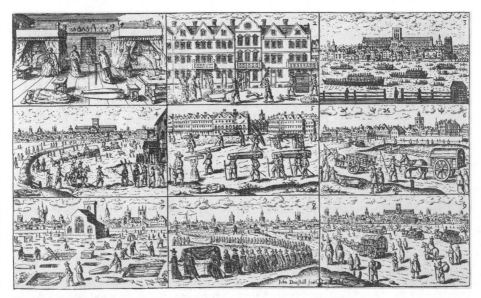

Figure 6.1 Plague scenes
Source: http://www.nationalarchives.gov.uk/education/lesson49.htm

There are three different types of plague and they are caused by a bacterial infection.

In London during 1665 the most common plague was the *Bubonic* type. The bacterium *Yersinia Pestis* is carried in the blood of infected black rats. Fleas living on the rats would carry a tiny amount of infected blood in their gut and would then infect any human unlucky enough to be bitten by them.

Once in the blood stream, the bacteria travel to the lymph glands in humans and cause painful swellings in the neck, armpit or groin. These are called *buboes* and are the body's defence mechanism trying to fight the infection. The buboes are extremely painful and would often become infected and covered with a livid red rash. Fever, weakness and sickness would quickly precede death, in many, but not all, victims.

Septicima plague is also contracted from an infected fleabite, but infects the victim's bloodstream, spreading through the whole body. As such it is invariably fatal, and swifter to claim its victim. Contact with open sores or bleeding spreads the disease to the next victim.

Pneumonic plague is the most deadly, and caused when the bacilli reach the lungs. Once there, pneumonia sets in, and coughs and sneezes spread infected droplets of water through the air to others. This is the most contagious of the three and the most easily spread.

Internal bleeding in all cases of plague infection caused large bruises to form on the skin, often in the fingertips, or toes, and it is this that gave rise to the name *Black Death*.

The Great Plague of 1665 was the biggest epidemic since the **Black Death** outbreak some 300 years before. It would eventually kill around 15 per cent of London's population – about 100,000 people.

The outbreak reputedly spread from Holland, arriving in London in May 1665 to the poor and overcrowded Parish of St-Giles-in-the-Field. As the plague took hold, measures were taken to try and contain the spread of the disease. People showing symptoms of the plague were taken to *pest houses* or *shut up* in their own dwellings along with any healthy members of their families. The door was nailed and locked, a red cross painted on it and no-one was permitted to leave for 40 days. After 40 days if anyone had survived, the red cross was replaced with a white one.

. . . This day, much against my Will, I did in Drury-lane see two or three houses marked with a red cross upon the doors, and 'Lord have mercy upon us' writ there – which was a sad sight to me, being the first of that kind that to my remembrance I ever saw. [1]

Each parish paid for *watchers* to guard the doors of *shut up* houses. Some people became paid *examiners* who reported ill people and families, while others became *scavengers* and *rakers,* responsible for clearing the houses and streets of the dead. There were even some who would enter houses as *nurses* or *searchers* to report on the health of the family and find out who had died.

Each week *Bills of Mortality* were posted that showed how many people had died. As the death toll mounted, those that could fled London to the countryside leaving the very poorest of the city to bear the brunt of the plague. Even the King and the Royal Court left, as did Parliament.

Theories regarding the causes of the plague abounded, along with cures to tackle the disease. Here are some of the commonly-held beliefs:

The plague is caused by *miasmas*, or mists in the air. Once it has been breathed in this poisoned air infects the body with the seeds of the pestilence.

People would cover their noses and mouths with masks or *nosegays* filled with herbs and sweet smelling flowers. Large fires and braziers were lit in streets to purify the air. Brimstone or sulphur was burnt and people would smoke tobacco in clay pipes to ward off the bad air.

That Fires in moveable Pans, or otherwise, be made in all necessary publique [public] Meetings in Churches, &c. and convenient Fumes to correct the Air be burnt thereon.

Orders for the prevention of the plague 1666, http://www.nationalarchives.gov.uk/education/lesson49.htm

---

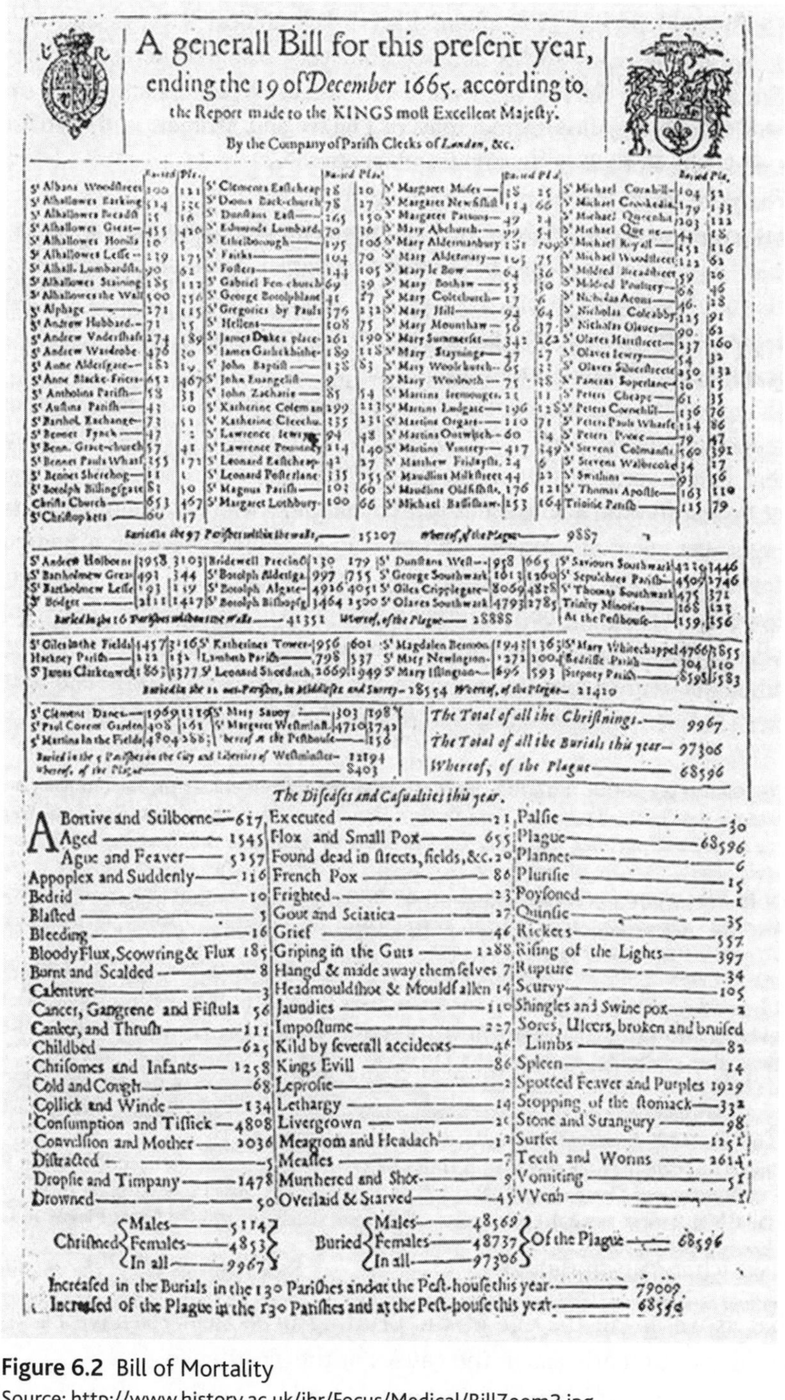

A generall Bill for this present year, ending the 19 of *December* 1665. according to the Report made to the KINGS most Excellent Majesty.

By the Company of Parish Clerks of *London*, &c.

Buried in the 97 Parishes within the walls, — 15207 *Whereof, of the Plague* — 9887

Buried in the 16 Parishes without the walls — 41351 *Whereof, of the Plague* — 28888

Buried in the 12 out-Parishes, in Middlesex and Surrey — 18554 *Whereof, of the Plague* — 21420

The Total of all the Christnings — 9967

The Total of all the Burials this year — 97306

Whereof, of the Plague — 68596

The Diseases and Casualties this year.

Abortive and Stilborne	617	Executed	21	Palsie	30
Aged	1545	Flox and Small Pox	655	Plague	68596
Ague and Feaver	5257	Found dead in streets, fields, &c.	20	Plannet	6
Appoplex and Suddenly	116	French Pox	86	Plurisie	15
Bedrid	10	Frighted	23	Poysoned	1
Blasted	5	Gout and Sciatica	27	Quinsie	35
Bleeding	16	Grief	46	Rickets	557
Bloody Flux, Scowring & Flux	185	Griping in the Guts	1288	Rising of the Lights	397
Burnt and Scalded	8	Hangd & made away themselves	7	Rupture	34
Calenture	3	Headmouldshot & Mouldfallen	14	Scurvy	105
Cancer, Gangrene and Fistula	56	Jaundies	110	Shingles and Swine pox	2
Canker, and Thrush	111	Impostume	227	Sores, Ulcers, broken and bruised Limbs	82
Childbed	625	Kild by severall accidents	46	Spleen	14
Chrisomes and Infants	1258	Kings Evill	86	Spotted Feaver and Purples	1929
Cold and Cough	68	Leprosie	2	Stopping of the stomack	332
Collick and Winde	134	Lethargy	14	Stone and Strangury	98
Consumption and Tissick	4808	Livergrown	20	Surfet	1251
Convulsion and Mother	2036	Meagrom and Headach	12	Teeth and Worms	2614
Distracted	5	Measles	7	Vomiting	51
Dropsie and Timpany	1478	Murthered and Shot	9	Wenn	8
Drowned	50	Overlaid & Starved	45		

Christned: Males — 5114; Females — 4853; In all — 9967

Buried: Males — 48569; Females — 48737; In all — 97306. Of the Plague — 68596

Increased in the Burials in the 130 Parishes and at the Pest-house this year — 79009

Increased of the Plague in the 130 Parishes and at the Pest-house this year — 68590

Figure 6.2 Bill of Mortality

Source: http://www.history.ac.uk/ihr/Focus/Medical/BillZoom2.jpg

> **The plague is God's punishment for the unrepented sins and wickedness of the world.** No one is free from guilt – and even innocent people, like infants, had to suffer for the sins of others.
>
> Prayer, and more prayer, fasting, and observing all religious holidays and instructions were recommended, along with repentance and leading a life free from sin. No gambling, drinking, laziness or promiscuity was to be tolerated.
>
> **The plague is caused by the filth and squalor of the poor, along with their poor diet.**
>
> Houses must be kept clean and the poor must be stopped from travelling or leaving the city and confined to their parishes. The streets must be cleaned of excrement and rotting piles of rubbish – which were cleared by 'rakers'. People had to take more care over buying and selling food at market.
>
> *That care be taken that no unwholsom Meats, stinking Fish, Flesh, musty Corn, or any other unwholesome Food be exposed to sale in any Shops or Markets.*
>
> Orders for the prevention of the plague 1666, http://www.nationalarchives.gov.uk/education/lesson49.htm

> **The plague is caused by animals, in particular cats and dogs and other domestic creatures, and livestock.**
>
> *That no Swine, Dogs, Cats or tame Pigeons be permitted to pass up and down in Streets, or from house to house, in places Infected.*
>
> Orders for the prevention of the plague 1666, http://www.nationalarchives.gov.uk/education/lesson49.htm

Daniel Defoe estimated 200,000 cats and 40,000 dogs were killed in response to an order from the Lord Mayor for Londoners to kill any creatures they found on the streets.

Spend a few minutes reading through the contextual information before assigning each group a particular theory of the four 'causes':

- Poisoned air.
- A punishment from God.
- The filth of the poor people.
- Animals, such as cats and dogs.

Explain that as we are in the age of the printing press, leaflets have been printed presenting different theories as to the causes of the 'pestilence'.

Each group is to create their version of the leaflet, starting with a still image or tableau that captures the ideas behind the theory. Along with the image, they should include a spoken title and any other language that might appear on the 'leaflet'. This might include ideas or instructions on avoiding the plague. Tell the students that once the tableau is established at the start of the drama, they can add movement or gesture and language that will animate the image and make it more interesting to watch. The sequence can be symbolic or more abstract in style – featuring repetition, slow motion movement or figurative mime.

Remind the groups that the real causes of the plague were unknown, and cures and remedies ineffective. Tell the groups that as well as starting their sequence with a still image, they should return to that same image at the end of their piece.

Allow adequate working time for the groups to prepare their dramas, before arranging the groups into a large circle facing inwards. Starting with the first group, explain that you want them to create their tableau, then as you move towards them they can begin their language and any movement or action they have devised.

Once they have finished performing, move towards the next group who should quickly form their tableau and begin their sequence as you approach. Repeat this process until all the groups have had a chance to share their work. Discuss the work and evaluate the effectiveness of the images, movement and any language used.

Stage three

Tell the group that for the next task, you are going to read them three extracts from a novel called *A Journal of the Plague Year* written by Daniel Defoe. Explain that the book was written in 1722 and is a fictional account of the events in London during the epidemic. Daniel Defoe would have been five years old in 1665, so it is likely the book is based on notes his father made.

The first account details a meeting with a group of people on the street, convinced they are seeing some omen of doom in the clouds above them.

One time before the plague was begun (otherwise than as I have said in St Giles's), I think it was in March, seeing a crowd of people in the street, I joined with them to satisfy my curiosity, and found them all staring up into the air to see what a woman told them appeared plain to her, which was an angel clothed in white, with a fiery sword in his hand, waving it or brandishing it over his head. She described every part of the figure to the life, showed them the motion and the form, and the poor people came into it so eagerly, and with so much readiness; 'Yes, I see it all plainly,' says one; 'there's the sword as plain as can be.' Another saw the angel. One saw his very face, and cried out what a glorious creature he was! One saw one thing, and one another. I looked as earnestly as the rest, but perhaps not with so much willingness to be imposed upon; and I said, indeed, that I could see nothing but a white cloud, bright on one side by the shining of the sun upon the other part. The woman endeavoured to show it me, but could not make me confess that I saw it, which, indeed, if I had I must have lied. But the woman, turning upon me, looked in my face, and fancied I laughed, in which her imagination deceived her too, for I really did not laugh, but was very seriously reflecting how the poor people were terrified by the force of their own imagination. However, she turned from me, called me profane fellow, and a scoffer; told me that it was a time of God's anger, and dreadful judgements were approaching, and that despisers such as I should wander and perish.[2]

Eyam plague village

The second account describes a terrified family visited at suppertime by a neighbour suffering with the plague:

> *Another infected person came and knocked at the door of a citizen's house where they knew him very well; the servant let him in, and being told the master of the house was above, he ran up and came into the room to them as the whole family was at supper. They began to rise up, a little surprised, not knowing what the matter was; but he bid them sit still, he only came to take his leave of them. They asked him, 'Why, Mr—, where are you going?' 'Going,' says he; 'I have got the sickness, and shall die tomorrow night.' 'Tis easy to believe, though not to describe, the consternation they were all in. The women and the man's daughters, which were but little girls, were frighted almost to death and got up, one running out at one door and one at another, some downstairs and some upstairs, and getting together as well as they could, locked themselves into their chambers and screamed out at the window for help, as if they had been frighted out of their wits. The master, more composed than they, though both frighted and provoked, was going to lay hands on him and throw him downstairs, being in a passion; but then, considering a little the condition of the man and the danger of touching him, horror seized his mind, and he stood still like one astonished. The poor distempered man all this while, being as well diseased in his brain as in his body, stood still like one amazed. At length he turns round: 'Ay!' says he, with all the seeming calmness imaginable, 'is it so with you all? Are you all disturbed at me? Why, then I'll e'en go home and die there.'[3]*

The final account details some of the 'quack' medicines and cures that were peddled to the panic-stricken people of London:

> *On the other hand it is incredible and scarce to be imagined, how the posts of houses and corners of streets were plastered over with doctors' bills and papers of ignorant fellows, quacking and tampering in physic, and inviting the people to come to them for remedies, which was generally set off with such flourishes as these, viz.: 'Infallible preventive pills against the plague.' 'Neverfailing preservatives against the infection.' 'Sovereign cordials against the corruption of the air.' 'Exact regulations for the conduct of the body in case of an infection.' 'Anti-pestilential pills.' 'Incomparable drink against the plague, never found out before.' 'An universal remedy for the plague.' 'The only true plague water.' 'The royal antidote against all kinds of infection'; – and such a number more that I cannot reckon up; and if I could, would fill a book of themselves to set them down.[4]*

Working in the same groups as before, assign an account for each of them to re-enact. This means that some of the groups in the class will work on the same piece of text. Make it clear to everyone that they do not have to interpret the complete story, but should focus on one or two moments that they feel offers potential for dramatic action.

Encourage the groups to consider how they could express the innermost thoughts and feelings of those people depicted in their drama. For instance, the story could freeze at different points allowing individual characters to step out and briefly express their thoughts and feelings to the audience, before moving back into the action. Encourage each group to see their drama as a self-contained short scene that will form part of a dramatic *montage*.

Montage

This term originated in film, with the innovative work of Sergei Eisenstein in the early twentieth century, and in drama it refers to the way in which meaning is created, not through linear narrative, but through the sequential juxtaposition of autonomous moments or stage images. In theatre perhaps the most influential proponents of montage have been Bertolt Brecht and his contemporary, Erwin Piscator, who saw it as a means of creating 'alienation' in audiences so that they might be less likely to empathize – and thus lose critical judgement (see also p.74).

In the classroom, although often requiring careful choreography, montage effects can be highly engaging, leading students to a better understanding of abstract and non-linear forms of performance.

Allow around 20 minutes for the groups to prepare, before stopping them and sharing their work.

After the performances, ask the students if the pieces of drama captured the individual human stories behind the epidemic. Do they think that when people look back at catastrophic historical events – affecting thousands of people – that there is a tendency to forget the individuals involved?

Stage four

Finish the work on the London plague by asking the group to consider:

If you had been living in London at the time, what would have been your response to the epidemic?

Ask the students to list what they might do if they were in the predicament of the Londoners of the time.

The woodcut opposite shows a group of wealthy people leaving the city as Death looks on. Explain that some of those wealthy or well-connected enough to acquire a certificate of health fled immediately, leaving behind the poorest people, who were barred from travel, to bear the brunt of the illness.

Figure 6.3 Woodcut, printed 1630, depicting Londoners fleeing from an outbreak of plague in a cart
Source: http://www.bbc.co.uk/schools/gcsebitesize/history/shp/middleages/earlymodernpublichealthrev2.shtml

Section two – Eyam village

Stage one

Explain that our location is going to change and we are going to look at life in a much smaller community; but first you want them to watch something . . .

Project or print the image of the Hadfield's Cottage in Eyam, explaining that this re-enactment takes place in the cottage with the black door.

Figure 6.4 Plague house
Source: http://www.geograph.org.uk/photo/620398

With the students in a circle, re-enact the moment when the Eyam tailor, George Viccars, opens the package of cloth from London. Projecting the detail from the Plague Window in Eyam Church might add to your re-enactment. To add detail and establish more clearly the link between London and Eyam, it is useful to use the letter which was sent by the merchant (section one) during this task.

Figure 6.5 The Plague Window, 1985, by Alfred Fisher. St Lawrence Church, Eyam, Derbyshire
Source: http://www.flickr.com/photos/30120216@N07/4306908019/sizes/z/in/photostream/

As the material is unpacked, George realizes that the cloth has got wet from the journey. In order to avoid the cloth spoiling further he lights a fire and lays the rolls of cloth out to dry.

Allow the students to witness the moment: ask them to remember what happened – it will be useful for what follows.

Stage two

Explain that the next part of the drama will require the pupils to take on a role, and that you will also be taking on a role in the next activity.

Write the word *community* on the board and lead a discussion:

Eyam plague village

- *What is a community?*

- *What makes a community strong?*

What would happen if something terrible happened in a small community – how would people react? Would they support each other or look after their own interests?

Explain that the drama takes place in a small rural village at the same time as the previous London explorations, almost 350 years ago, in the year 1665. Our village is called Eyam (pronounced *E'em*) in Derbyshire, set deep in the rugged limestone hills and dales and around 12 miles from the city of Sheffield. There is a plentiful supply of water, and rich deposits of lead in the ground give employment to those willing to dig it out.

Ask the students to consider:

- *What do we know about life almost 350 years ago?*

- *If you were a villager, how would **you** make **your** living?*

Rural village life in the seventeenth century would have been very insular; villages and small towns would often be remote and would need to be largely self sufficient in terms of food and other supplies. People often lived and worked in large family units, and skills and trades would be passed down from father to son. Many villagers would have a small amount of rented land that they would farm when times were hard.

In our drama, explain that individual roles will be defined by their job. Some examples might be:

lead miner	blacksmith	butcher
shepherd	cowman	thatcher
potter	baker	glover
farm labourer	cordwainer (shoemaker)	basketmaker
candlemaker	brewer	weaver
painter	sexton (gravedigger)	wheelwright
cooper (barrel maker)	draper	saddler
tailor	milkmaid	tanner
merchant	mason	
miller	carpenter	

...these should offer lots of scope for students to begin to develop meaningful roles.

Occupations in the past

Most people will know what a *tailor, baker* or *potter* does for a living, but what about a *sexton* or a *cordwainer*?

Research any occupations with which you are unfamiliar. Are you aware of any other occupations which have now virtually died out?

Do any of the people in your class have family names which relate to occupations? Surnames first appeared in this country after the Norman Conquest in 1066 and are often derived from places where people lived, their occupation or even a nickname used to describe a person's distinctive appearance. As names began to be passed down from generation to generation, sometimes they were changed or mis-recorded. Smith is the most common surname in the UK and is derived from the occupation of blacksmith.

Ask the students to get into small groups of around 3 or 4, which will represent family units in the next stage of the drama. Advise the students that they can take on the roles of children – but that the children should be at least 12 years old if the drama is to maintain its integrity!

Each family group needs to be identified by a profession or trade from the list provided.

Explain that for the next part of the drama, the whole group will be working in role. If necessary, remind them that this means adopting the thoughts, opinions and ideas of the person they are depicting, and behaving as if they live in the past. Ask the groups to find their own space in the room, and to create a still image or tableau of the family going about their daily activities. In this way the class will be building a composite picture or snapshot of village life on a busy working day. Explain that it is morning on a warm, late summer day. Allow a minute for preparation, and then freeze the group.

While the group hold their still images, explain that you will 'travel around the village' asking questions directly to individuals. Inexperienced students may need reminding that they should answer in the first person: *I am . . . or I feel . . .*

Quickly travel around the village asking questions of individuals – reinforcing belief in their roles and building a deeper understanding of the context of the drama, and creating a sense of the emerging fictional community.

- *What are you selling?*
- *Are you making something?*
- *That looks like hard work?*
- *Is that a heavy load you are carrying?*
- *Is this a good village to live in?*
- *Do you know most of the people who live here?*
- *How long has your family lived in the village?*

After questioning individuals in the groups in this manner explain that the village is briefly going to 'come to life', with the intention that the dramatic context of the village – and the roles the students are playing within it – can be developed through mime and movement.

Using *parallel play* – where each group works individually without interacting with their neighbour – start the groups' improvisations with a countdown. This ensures spontaneous (rather than composed) improvisation – which students should find provides a natural extension to the previous exercise.

Count the students in and allow them a few minutes to establish the dramatic action of their improvisation. Stop the work and explain that for the next part of the drama, you will be taking on a role and joining in with the (replayed) improvisations the groups have just created. The students will have to listen carefully and try to establish the context of your role, and react in role accordingly.

Improvisation and composition

Improvisation is a much used and much debated term in drama education. Strictly speaking, improvisation is spontaneous 'composition through performance' as in the case of 'free' jazz musicians. However, in most examples in the arts, 'improvisation' takes place within a clear structure, and follows relatively familiar patterns, as in a rock guitarist's solo, or within a semi-improvised *Lazzi* in *Commedia dell'Arte*.

In drama education, some confusion has been caused through the widespread (and oxymoronic) use of the term *prepared (or polished) improvisation*, which usually refers to short pieces of drama that are devised in small groups for classroom presentation to an audience, often of peers. This process – referred to by Jonathan Neelands[5] as *Small Group Playmaking*, whilst being improvised in the sense that it is 'made up' – need not necessarily entail any true improvisation at all.

What is important here is that teachers and students are clear about the purpose of the activities they are undertaking, and the dramatic 'mode' within which they are operating: prepared improvisation is most often used as part of a devising process – to generate material for performance, in which case the students are working in a performance orientation: their work is designed for an audience, and therefore they will legitimately attend to the 'stagecraft' and technique of their work, necessary to create a satisfying experience for those witnessing it.

However, in many drama lessons spontaneous improvisation is used *experientially* to facilitate exploration of a particular dramatic context, either as rehearsal tool to enable performers to gain insight into the character they are playing, or in the form of structured role-play, as a means of 'living through' a fictional moment. In this *experiential mode*,[6] participants are not attempting to compose drama that will be performed later to an audience: they are 'in the moment'; it is therefore not legitimate to challenge them for their perceived lack of skill as performers!

In the Eyam unit, we move quite freely from one 'mode' to the other: students might be asked to compose a short drama which is then interrupted by a teacher working in role – thus transforming it from 'performative' to 'experiential' mode, or might create a spontaneous drama which they then edit and re-model *as performance*.

In each case, the demands made on students are quite different, as are the learning outcomes of the particular activities.

Choosing one of the groups to begin, ask them to get ready to replay their improvisation. Once they have established their drama, enter in role as George Viccars, the local tailor who has some recently-arrived cloth from London to sell. It is very useful at this stage to have a roll or sample of cloth to act as a role signifier and prop.

Good day sir, madam,

As you know, I work and lodge with the Hadfields in the village. George Viccars is the name. A tailor by trade, and wonder if anyone in your household might be interested in commissioning a beautiful garment or suit of clothes to be fashioned from the very finest cloth newly arrived from London?

I can assure you of the highest quality of craftsmanship and attention to detail ... perhaps for the lady of the house ... the gentleman? Would you like to inspect my sample here, as you can see a lovely colour and delightful weave ...

Once the first group has had a chance to interact with you in role, co-ordinate the same performance with every group. Will anyone buy the cloth – perhaps to make a dress for a wedding or a very special garment? It has come *all the way from London and is of the finest quality ...*

Once all the groups have had a chance to interact with the tailor explain that the work can move forward in time by a few days. Ask the students to re-establish their family units, as the next improvisation will occur at home in the evening, at supper-time. Once the students have defined their space, ask one of them who is playing an adult to come to you to be 'briefed' separately.

Once you have a representative from each group around you, quickly and quietly give them the following information.

There has been some news in the village.

I heard earlier today that poor George Viccars, the tailor, has passed away. He had developed a fever some days before and taken to his bed. His illness grew worse until finally he died, it is very sad news – but not particularly unusual in this day and age.

Tell them that this is a piece of information you want them to include in their drama. In addition, remind them that the plague – about which the villagers might have heard news – was largely confined to London (although some northern cities, such as York, might have experienced some deaths). Plague was unheard-of in small villages.

Start off the groups with a countdown – again as *spontaneous* improvisation. At the end of the working time ask them to review their drama and choose a significant moment to develop into a more polished scene, thus moving from a spontaneous mode of working into a prepared and rehearsed performance.

Allow a further 10 or 15 minutes for the groups to prepare their work, before sharing. Discuss and evaluate the work. In the dramas:

- What conclusions, if any, did the villagers come to?
- Is George's death simply a tragic event?
- Does anyone know what he died of?

Eyam plague village

Figure 6.6 The Plague Window, 1985, by Alfred Fisher. St Lawrence Church, Eyam, Derbyshire
Source: http://www.flickr.com/photos/30120216@N07/4306909441/sizes/z/in/photostream/

Stage three

Narrate the next piece of information:

Time has passed on and it is four weeks after the unfortunate death of the tailor. As it is Sunday, the villagers have gathered inside the church doors before the morning service.

Project or print off the picture of the church in Eyam.

Ask the group to describe their ideas of the typical interior layout of a church.

- Where would they expect the congregation to sit?

- From where would they expect the rector or vicar to deliver the sermon?

Ask the group to quickly define the space in that manner using chairs or stage blocks.

Figure 6.7 Eyam Church
Source: http://www.geograph.org.uk/photo/21749

Next ask them to take their places as members of the congregation, sitting in their family units.

For this next whole-group role-play, you will again need to brief some members of the class separately. Using the role information cards, invite five students to come forward from the main group. Distribute the five information cards and check for understanding.

Explain to the five students that you want them to use this information to develop the role-play you are about to start. Tell them that they should not simply read out the card – but they should try to capture the essence of what the card is saying. They can elaborate or add other information if they wish – within the limits of their role.

Role Card 1

Years ago you went to London. You saw a victim of the plague there. They were coughing and feverish and had weeping sores all over their body. You think that this is what has killed your neighbours and friends. It is true – the plague has come to your village.

Role Card 2

You remember your grandfather telling you of a terrible illness. He called it *the plague*. He said that once you were taken ill, you started to cough blood. Then enormous swellings grew under your arms and on your neck – until they burst. Death followed soon after. There is no cure.

113

Role Card 3

You know why the plague has come to your village. You remember a few months ago when some cows were lured into the church as a practical joke. Surely that would have displeased God – this is his punishment. We should punish the ones who played the prank.

Role Card 4

You know why the plague has come to your village. You have heard the terrible sounds of *Gabriel Hounds* hovering over the moor near the village. These are the spirits of unbaptized children. This is why the plague has come to your village.

Role Card 5

You know why the plague has come to your village. White crickets have been seen on the moors and everyone knows that means the village will be visited by some great tragedy. The village is to be tested over the next few months as the bad luck takes over.

Figure 6.8 The Plague Window, 1985, by Alfred Fisher. St Lawrence Church, Eyam, Derbyshire
Source: http://www.flickr.com/photos/30120216@N07/4306904197/sizes/z/in/photostream/

Ask the students to re-join their groups, and when they have taken their place, explain that you will be taking on the role of William Mompesson – the village rector – who will conduct the service.

Start the role-play by asking the 'congregation' to rise; then, as they sit, begin the sermon:

It is heartening to see so many of the village here this morning. As you know I am William Mompesson, and along with my wife and two children I consider myself very much part of village life here in Eyam, even though we have only been here for little over a year. It is therefore with a heavy heart that I have to tell you all of the sudden and unaccountable deaths of several of our parishioners.

In total, seven people have died in the last two weeks, in the most sudden and surprising circumstances. It seems an illness has struck that quickly carries those stricken off to God's mercy. I fear that there are others ill – at home and too weak to come to church.

My heart is heavy and I feel we face some terrible trial. We should pray for God's forgiveness and mercy. I would like to offer the chance for others in the village to share their views on this matter.

Invite responses from the congregation, prompting the students who have been given role-cards to contribute.

Running the whole-group role play will allow the students to gradually realize that the plague has come to 'their' village.

Some contextual prompts that you might want to build in to your responses in this section:

- If they leave, they leave behind *everything* they own. Only the very wealthy could afford to do that.

- Only a minority of people would have travelled far outside the village. Where would they go, if they left?

- If they leave, and go to another village, they risk spreading the plague to their neighbours.

- Once the neighbouring villages know about the plague, would anyone from Eyam be made welcome?

At the end of the sermon, dismiss the churchgoers, entreating them to go back to their houses and consider their options.

Out of role, ask the students to consider how the villagers might have felt. Remind them that as the plague was largely confined to large cities, individual experience of dealing with the illness would have been rare, and ignorance about the causes of the disease would have made the prospect of living in close proximity to a plague sufferer terrifying.

Eyam plague village

Stage four

Ask the students to return to their family groups.

The day passed slowly, children that would normally be playing outside were kept indoors; neighbours kept themselves to themselves; doors and windows were shut. As evening approached, and the children were sent to bed, in hushed tones the families discussed what to do.

Ask them to divide their family group based on age. The parents or older villagers are discussing what they think the family should do; the children have been sent to bed, but are aware that something serious is happening.

Explain that you would like each half of the family to compose a separate short improvisation that represents the families' thoughts and feelings about what might happen to them.

Propose introducing some conflict and dramatic tension into the drama by suggesting that the parents might be disagreeing with each other on the best thing to do: perhaps the father wants to leave while the mother feels that staying in the village – and trusting in providence – might be the best course of action. In contrast, the children might be scaring each other with stories they may have heard, or be simply saying their prayers.

Allow around 10 minutes for the work to develop, before introducing the concept of *split stage*. Tell the groups that they need to select two or three points in their drama when one side of the stage 'freezes' and the other side becomes the focus of the audience. In this way, the drama cuts from side to side, highlighting contrasts in the way older and younger members of the family are responding to their dilemma.

Once the groups have had the chance to rehearse their split stage drama, share each group's work in turn.

In between each group's performance add the following narration, to signify the passing of time:

In October and November 1665, a further 28 people died in Eyam.

In December and January, 1666, 12 people.

In February and March and April, 14 perished.

In May, only two deaths were reported. The village breathed a sigh of relief; perhaps the pestilence had left them?

In June, as the warm weather returned: 21 deaths.

Stage five

Once all the groups have shared the work, ask the students to re-form the shape of the church, tell them that at this church service they are to receive more news from Mompesson, the rector.

Once the space has been defined, call the meeting to order in role as Mompesson. The following address will set up the discussion:

My fellow villagers.

We know now we are in the grip of a dreadful pestilence that seems unwilling to grant us mercy. I have, along with Thomas Stanley my much-loved colleague and predecessor here at the church in Eyam, devised a plan.

This will be the last time the church will be used for service. Instead we will meet collectively in the clean fresh air of Cucklet Delf: the steep slopes will provide shelter, and form the perfect setting for worship.

Secondly, families must take responsibility for burying their own dead, on their own land – or in nearby fields. Internment must follow immediately after death. Where there is no family member remaining, an appointed villager will enter the dwelling and take the unfortunate to his or her final resting place.

Finally – lest we spread this dreadful disease to our neighbours, we propose a cordon-sanitaire be set around the village – whereby no villager shall leave the boundary, and no visitor shall enter until such times as the village is deemed clear of the illness. Already I have secured the help of the Earl of Devonshire who promises to arrange supplies to be left at the well and other boundary markers. I am sure our neighbours will help us in our hour of need, considering the sacrifice we are making to spare them from our fate.

How say you? Would you promise to such a thing? Are you willing to make such a sacrifice and place your fate in the hands of God? The cordon will only work if we all take an oath to stay.

I'm sure you have much to say, who will speak first?

Allow the students to respond in role. At the end of the role-play, freeze the action and ask each student – still in role – to speak a few words that expresses their thoughts or feelings about what is happening to their village. (*Thought-tracking.*)

> There are no first-hand accounts of how the villagers reacted to the proposed self-quarantine, but all the villagers must have been aware of the potential risks in staying. By this stage some villagers had already fled, Mompesson himself had sent his own two children away and unsuccessfully tried to convince his wife Katherine to leave as well. Despite their fear, the remaining villagers chose to stay and contain the disease at great personal cost. There are accounts of only two people breaking the cordon, once it had been established.

Stage six

The next few exercises are small-group *prepared improvisations*. Each one is based on a story or account from Eyam. This will give students an opportunity to work in different groups and leave the roles they have established over the last few tasks.

These prepared improvisations could be explored in a number of ways. Working in small groups, the whole class could be tasked to work on the same stimulus and develop different versions of the same event. Alternatively, the class could be divided into groups working on different accounts, before sharing their drama in a *performance cycle*.

The story of Emmott Sydall and Rowland Torre

Emmott, a village girl, and her mother were the only surviving members of her family; having lost her father, brother and four sisters in April 1665. Rowland lived in neighbouring Middleton-Dale and before the plague had come, had asked her to marry him. As betrothed sweethearts, and before the cordon was established, Rowland Torre would visit Emmott at her home and later in secret at Cucklet Delf, calling to each other over the river. Eventually, Emmott convinced Rowland that their meetings must cease until the plague had left the village.

One day in April, Emmott succumbed to the disease and died, leaving a heartbroken Rowland an agonizing wait before he eventually found out what had happened to her and entered the village to visit her grave.

Dramatic focus: Emmott and Rowland exchanging promises to wait until the plague had left the village;

Rowland's family telling him to stay away from Eyam;

Meeting secretly at Cucklet Delf

Emmott convincing Rowland not to visit her anymore;

Rowland discovering Emmott has died.

Figure 6.9 The Plague Window, 1985, by Alfred Fisher. St Lawrence Church, Eyam, Derbyshire
Source: http://www.flickr.com/photos/30120216@N07/4306905547/sizes/z/in/photostream/

Margaret Blackwell's story

Margaret Blackwell was 18 years old when she became ill with the plague. Having already lost all her family apart from her brother, she was gripped at night with a fever. In the morning, her brother, suspecting the worst for his sister, had left the house early.

Margaret woke some time later with a raging thirst and racked with illness. Searching desperately for water, she instead found the fat from the cooked bacon that her brother had left in a wooden cup or 'piggin'. Mistaking it for water, she drained the cup in one go and returned to her bed. When her brother apprehensively returned from his journey of fetching coal he expected to find her dead, but instead found her much recovered.

Dramatic focus: Margaret's brother attempting to wake his sister before realizing she was ill; the brother leaving the house, telling a neighbour of his ill sister; Margaret drinking the bacon fat; the brother, returning to the house some hours later, finds Margaret alive and well.

The boundary stone

Figure 6.10 Boundary stone
Source: http://www.flickr.com/photos/81538501@N00/2227501487/

Tradition has it that supplies and provisions were left for the Eyam villagers by their grateful neighbours at boundary stones or at Mompesson's Well. Payment was left in the drilled holes in the stone and the coins covered with vinegar or pepper. Coins placed in the well were thought to be washed clean of the seeds of plague by the running water.

Eyam plague village

> **Dramatic focus:** a small group of Eyam villagers wait by the boundary stone or well, as some neighbours leave food and medicine: what do they say to each other? Do the neighbours appreciate what the Eyam villagers are doing for them? Are there any messages passed on to friends and family on either side of the cordon?

Unwin of the Townhead's story

Marshall Howe became the village's unofficial sexton and gravedigger after each family was ordered to be responsible for burying their own dead. Marshall had contracted the disease early on in the outbreak but had survived and as such he thought himself immune.

His service – of removing bodies – was much in demand, and if he cleared the last family member from a house, he helped himself to their belongings in payment for his services.

On this occasion, it happened that a man called Unwin lay dead or dying in his house. After digging a shallow grave on the premises, Marshall Howe went inside to carry or drag the body out. He was halfway down the stairs with the unfortunate on his back, when Unwin cried out 'I want a possett' – a milk drink with bread and ale. Marshall put the man down and left in indignation. Unwin went on to make a full recovery.

> **Dramatic focus:** Marshall digging a shallow grave for Unwin; Marshall entering the house and dragging him out; the man awakening and his family rushing to help him as Marshall leaves.

Tideswell market

Tideswell was the principal market town for Eyam, located as it was about five miles west of the village. As so many were concerned about the plague in Eyam spreading, a watchguard was put on the eastern entrance to the town to question strangers and stop any Eyam residents from entering.

A lady of Eyam, however, decided to journey to the market and when she was accosted by the guard, she explained she was from Orchard Bank – a part of Eyam. When asked where Orchard Bank was by the guard, she replied 'why verily, it is in the land of the living.' The guard let her pass, not knowing where Orchard Bank was. It was only a few moments later though that the woman was recognized and a great cry went up 'The plague! The plague! A woman from Eyam!'

The woman was chased out of the market by an angry mob hurling rocks, sticks and mud.

> **Dramatic focus**: the woman being questioned by the watchguard; the woman being recognized; the angry mob driving the woman out of the market; the angry mob confronting the hapless watchguard; the woman returning home and being questioned by the Eyam villagers.

Allow around 20 minutes for the groups to prepare their improvisations. Define a performance area and present each drama in turn.

In between each group's performance add the following narration:

In July 1666, 56 were taken by the plague.

In August 1666, 78 died.

In September 1666, 24 deaths

In October the numbers dropped further, to 18.

The final recorded death was Abraham Morten, on 1 November 1666.

At last the village was plague free.

No one died of the plague anywhere else in Derbyshire: the villagers' sacrifice
*   succeeded in preventing the spread of the disease.*

But at a cost: in total, 260 people died.

Stage seven

Display the images of the stained glass windows in Eyam church, made by Alfred Fisher in 1985, which commemorate the villagers.

In groups of four, ask the students to create their own memorial to the people of Eyam. This could take the form of:

- A sequence of *tableaux vivants* based on the stained glass windows, with spoken 'captions'.

- A 'statue' erected to the villagers in the town square, again, with a spoken 'inscription'.

- A ritual which might take place once a year by the boundary stone in Eyam, in which names of the plague victims (some of them!) are intoned: http://www.eyamplaguevillage.co.uk/index.php/eyam-plague/plague-victims

Present the work as a means of facilitating reflection on the whole project.

The resources for this Unit are available for download at www.routledge.com/9780415572064

Wordless books

Thematic content in this unit:	Curriculum connections:
Discrimination and cultural division	History, Citizenship, PHSE
Colonization	History, Economics, Citizenship
Propaganda	History, Media Studies, Art & Design
Graphic novels, comics and wordless books	Art and Graphic Design, English, Media Studies
Script writing and devising	English, Drama

Dramatic techniques and keywords in this unit:	
Scripting	Genre
Drafting and redrafting	Flashback
Narrative	Plot
Content	Form

This unit explores the use of wordless books (books that use pictures to tell a story), first as a stimulus for creating scripted and improvised drama, and then as a cross-curricular resource exploring issues of prejudice and cultural oppression. Wordless books, or 'graphic novels', have long been used in the classroom with younger students as an aid to developing literacy, and their use is increasing as an accessible and stimulating resource for students learning English as an additional language.

The wordless book we have chosen to work with is *Red Shoes*[1] by Mandy Coe, which is easily available and suitable for older students. We believe, however, that the basic structure outlined below would be adaptable to other works perhaps more suitable for younger or less-experienced students. *Red Shoes* is a 'novel' composed of cartoon-style images with no written text. It shows how the 'Red Shoes' are forced to leave their own land when it is colonized by the 'Black Shoes'. Images of discrimination and cultural division are interspersed with sketches showing people meeting, seemingly in secret, to tell their tales. The implication is that the Red Shoe people's language has been made illegal and that they 'speak in pictures'.

Where this unit connects

In its theme this work clearly connects with historic and contemporary examples of discrimination and cultural division, although the power of 'Red Shoes' seems to be in its ability to cross contexts, and relating the work too early or too strongly to any particular socio-political context may be counter-productive. Nevertheless there are clear resonances within *Red Shoes* to apartheid-era South Africa, Northern Ireland and the segregated states of the USA, as well as to literary sources such as Orwell's *1984* and to Swift's *Gulliver's Travels*.

Students will probably be familiar with the use of the comic-book format to deal with 'serious' topics – as in Art Spiegelman's Pullitzer Prize-winning *Maus,* or comic-book retellings of Shakespeare's plays. *Red Shoes* also relates to an earlier tradition of graphic novels – popular in the middle years of the twentieth century – which use stark, high-quality images (often woodcuts or linoprints influenced by medieval prints) to carry a narrative with no, or few, words. Notable examples are *White Collar*[2] by Giacomo Patri (1938), which we have also used as a basis for drama, or *Passionate Journey* by Frans Masereel (1926), acknowledged as the master of this genre.

Working in drama: by the end of this unit students will have:

- Used a range of techniques, including composing songs and poems, to bring to life the 'world' of the book.

- Used visual images to devise scripted and improvised drama.

- Created 'propaganda', and considered appropriate forms of drama for influencing others.

- Used drama techniques to create the character of 'Jo', and used the form to explore the consequences of political and moral choices on individuals.

Section one – The Black Shoes

In order to capture the imagination of the group and begin the exploration, read through the following extract and proceed straight into the consolidating exercise.

Wordless books

Anthropologists have just discovered some startling evidence surrounding a previously unreported society we shall call the 'Black Shoes'. Life in this community was evidently rich and full of culture, art and commerce. Hard work and endeavour were well rewarded, with some enjoying substantial rewards and living lives of considerable ease. As well as these privileged few, those in need were looked after and no-one went hungry and no-one went cold. Shelter was provided for those who had none, and care offered for those too ill to work to support themselves. The leaders of the land were elected by vote and in this democratic world, laws were passed to protect people, property and personal freedom. In order to keep themselves safe, the Black Shoes built barriers and gates to stop others taking advantage of their prosperous world. Some of these people began to look on with envy at the high walls, and the type of life that lay behind them. The Black Shoes would trade and conduct business with their neighbours and many Black Shoes left and went elsewhere, building empires and businesses. People wrote songs of the beautiful life the Black Shoes led and the Black Shoes had a poem/song/motto that summed up their life. The first four lines of the poem/song were/the motto was . . .

In small groups of four or five, ask the students to compose the first four lines of the song. The song should attempt to capture the essence of the wonderful life the Black Shoes enjoyed. Each line could contain a specific idea to show how wonderful this society truly is. For example:

Our Black Shoe world is full of choice

From child to adult, find your voice!

For those too ill we will look after

Our pleasant land so rich in laughter.

Students could design a flag that goes with their national song and prepare a rendition to be presented to the rest of the group.

Section two – Red and Black

Stage one

Allow students to study Image 1:

Image 1

Ask the students, in groups, to speculate about the image:

- Who is the person carrying the suitcases?
- Where might these events be taking place?
- Why is he/she there?
- What is the significance of the references to Red/Black shoes?

After sharing the groups' findings, ask them to record, using 'post-it' notes, the possible thoughts, feelings – or words actually spoken – of the people in the image. These can be attached to the image in the form of 'speech bubbles'. If appropriate this can be scripted as a sequence of dialogues between the various people in the scene.

Still working in groups, tell the students that they are to present their 'dialogues' as a sequence of short dramatic presentations. Ask the students to study the picture again and identify one of the people to characterize physically. Ask them to try and

Wordless books

capture the shape and posture of the person and to see their character as part of the complete image. This still image will act as the frame from which to share the language work. More sophisticated students might wish to subtly change the image as each person says their lines, resulting in a more animated image: do any of the character relationships change in this short sequence? How does the final image compare with the image they started from?

At this early stage in the work these fragmentary dramas do not have to 'make sense'; it may be wise to discourage students from imposing a fixed narrative and meaning too early. Ask the students to reflect on their work so far: what might the 'world' of the Black Shoes be like? What else might go on there? What might it feel like to be a 'Red Shoe' in a 'Black Shoe' world?

Stage two

In the same groups, ask the students to create 30-second scenes showing what kinds of things might happen to 'Jo', the person with the suitcases, on the day that he/she arrives.

After sharing the work, present the sequence of Images (2, 3, 4 and 5):

What do these images tell us about the world that Jo has come to? What questions do they raise?

Image 2

Image 3

Image 4

Image 5

In groups ask the students to build on their previous dramas by creating short scenes based on one of the images; each must include the character of Jo somehow – even if he/she is just an onlooker. Each drama should end with a spoken line – dialogue or thought – in the form of a question; perhaps something that the students would like to explore later in the unit. Share the work.

Stage three

Working solo, in role as a migrant 'Red Shoe' like Jo, ask each student to write a letter to a close friend or relative back home in 'Red Shoe' land. Ask each student to conclude their letter with the sentence, 'I include a ——— in the hope that you will not forget me'. Each student should choose a small object which might be included in the letter home as a token of remembrance.

Once the task is complete, share the 'messages home' by presenting them (or edited phrases from them) as a sequence, ending with the 'I include . . .' sentence, to create a kind of fragmentary diary or poem based on Jo's experience as a recent migrant to 'Black Shoe' land. Encourage the group to develop a ritual quality – perhaps in the way they intone the lines – and 'place' the symbolic objects.

Stage four

Ask students to form groups of four, and to swap their letters with another group. Explain that as 'Red Shoe' culture is suppressed by the Black Shoes, any explicit criticism of Black Shoes in the messages home will be censored!

Change the drama 'frame' by addressing the students in role as the Black Shoe 'Chief of Police':

We have been monitoring the mail of some recent Red Shoe arrivals believed to be subversives . . . now, your task is to check these letters and postcards, and identify any potential suspects.

Working in role as 'secret police' ask the students to highlight anything that could be construed as criticism of Black Shoes.

Conclude the section by remarking (still in role as the Chief of Police), 'any guilty subversives will be rounded up and dealt with . . .'

Out of role, encourage the students to reflect on their work so far:

- What might happen to the 'subversive' Red Shoes?

- If you knew that you were being constantly monitored, what effect would that have on you?

- Can we summarize what we now know about the Black Shoe people? Why do they behave in the way they do?

Changing perspective or 'frame'

One of the obvious advantages of working in dramatic form is that it enables shifts in perspective: participants are able to view events or issues from different viewpoints. Often, as in the case above, the shift can be quite sudden and can provide a productive tension between quite opposing positions or ideologies, it can challenge students' assumptions or clarify their own feelings and values.

The notion of *dramatic frame* is useful here. A frame in drama defines the parameters of a given fictional situation – on one level, what Stanislavski might have referred to as the *given circumstances* within which the fiction is to operate. It defines participants' roles in the drama but also suggests a perspective or attitude to the depicted events, and poses possible questions or lines of enquiry. The choice of frame – in a classroom drama, as in a scripted play created by a playwright, is crucial to the outcomes of the drama.

Wordless books

> For instance, in a drama about the death of a homeless person on the street there are many possible dramatic frames available:
>
> - In terms of **role** and **focus**, participants could take on the role of the homeless themselves; welfare workers trying to ensure that such a thing doesn't happen again; the police sent to investigate the incident; families of those living on the street in search of justice; a TV crew creating a controversial documentary (etc.);
>
> - In terms of **chronology,** the drama could be taking place at the time of the death; living through the events that led up to the death, or in the time after the death, viewing the incident as an historical event (etc.);
>
> - In terms of **geography,** participants could be physically near to the event (as in a drama taking place on the street itself) or distant from it – (with characters watching a report about the event on television).
>
> Thinking about planning a drama in this way can be fascinating; as can be demonstrated, there are many possible combinations of these framing factors, and each will produce a different dramatic encounter, a different experience, different challenges and different outcomes.
>
> One key factor to take into account is *frame distance*[3]: some choices of dramatic frame will position the participants in the drama 'close' to the action – not necessarily physically, but emotionally – whilst others are more likely to encourage 'cooler', more objective, and perhaps safer, responses. Cooler frames are often most productive, particularly when working with inexperienced students in naturalistic improvised drama: distance – as Brecht reminds us – can also be a product of choosing the appropriate *form* for the drama.

Section three – propaganda

> **Propaganda:** a form of communication that is aimed at influencing the attitude of a community toward some cause or position . . .

Stage one

Present Images 6, 7, 8 and 9:

Image 6

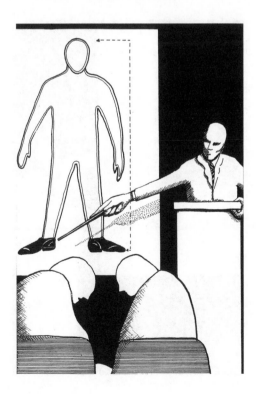

Image 7

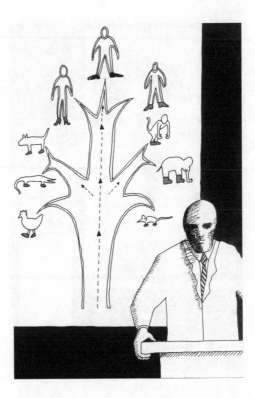

Image 8

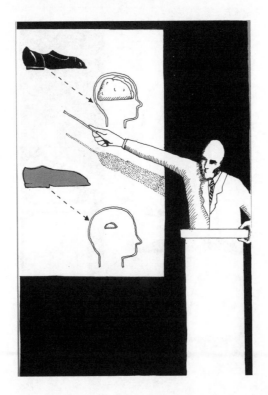

Image 9

Ask the class for responses to these images:

- Who is the person at the lectern?
- What are the images trying to communicate, and to whom?
- In the case of the Black Shoe people, what effect would such propaganda have? How might it make them behave towards the Red Shoes?

Can the students think of real-life examples of similar *propaganda*?

Stage two

Present these quotations to the class:

> 1 *History is the version of past events that people have decided to agree upon.*
>
> 2 *If you tell a big enough lie and tell it frequently enough, it will be believed.*
>
> 3 *People can be made to see paradise as hell, and also the other way around: to consider the most wretched sort of life as paradise.*
>
> 4 *Prejudice, not being founded on reason, cannot be removed by argument.*

Ask the students to explore the quotations for meaning, and to create group images that illustrate possible meanings. (The students may be interested to learn that the fourth quotation is from Samuel Johnson and the first from Napoleon Bonaparte; quotations two and three are Adolf Hitler!)

After appropriate working time, share.

Stage three

In groups of four or five ask the students to devise a short (30 seconds) propaganda piece which the people in Image 10 might be watching.

Ask the class to consider an appropriate dramatic style for their work: for instance are they going to address the 'audience' directly, or use a more *naturalistic* style?

Will they – in the style of TV documentary – use interviews with people to make their points? What about the use of statistics?

Some effective propaganda uses an 'indirect' method of creating meaning by using strong visual images with particular associations for the people watching – an example might be the use of a flag, landscape or iconic book.

Image 10

Section four – Jo's story

Stage one

Re-introduce Image 5 – of 'Jo' in prison. Ask the students, working in groups of four, to add Jo's thoughts and feelings to the image using 'post-it' notes. Use these starting points:

- *I wish . . .*
- *I hope . . .*
- *The thing I miss most is . . .*
- *If I could change one thing it would be . . .*
- *When I get out I . . .*

Explain that they are going to create a short drama, which explores how Jo came to be in prison, and what happened after Jo was released. All groups will start from the same starting point – based on the previous exercise.

Ask the students to select one member of each group to represent Jo in the prison cell. Other members of the group speak his thoughts – in the form of the lines written in the previous exercise. Encourage them to build atmosphere and tension – perhaps to create Jo's sense of longing for freedom.

Stage two

From this starting point, ask the groups to create further scenes: the first uses *flashback* to show how Jo came to be in prison.

Ask the students to consider how they might alert an audience to the fact that the action is shifting to another time; in film this is straightforward and easily recognizable, but how might the same information be conveyed in live drama?

Chronology in drama: *Flashback*

In ***flashback***, the chronological sequence of a piece of drama is interrupted in order to present events that occurred prior to the main time sequence of the work.

It is very commonly used in film and TV, and students will be familiar with the clichéd filmic conventions used in old films to signal flashbacks: the screen becoming 'wary' and distorted; the days falling from the calendar; the use of black and white in an otherwise colour film (and vice-versa); or a particular piece of music, often distorted, associated with the protagonist's early life, etc.

On stage, notable examples of playwrights handling chronology in interesting ways can be found in:

Bertolt Brecht: *The Caucasian Chalk Circle* – in which two separate narratives concerning different main characters unfold sequentially, before the two characters finally meet in the last act of the play.

Arthur Miller: *Death of a Salesman* – where Willy Loman has 'time shifts' within the play – scenes begin in the present but characters are present on stage that only he (and, of course, the audience) can see and hear.

Harold Pinter: *Betrayal* – which actually uses 'reverse chronology'; the story is told from 'end' to 'beginning'!

Stage three

The second scene moves the action into the future: once released we see Jo meet with another character or characters, in secret.

- Who might the character(s) be?
- Why are they meeting in secret?
- To do what?

Wordless books

Once rehearsed, experiment with running the scenes in various sequences; which is most effective?

Is it possible to move from the prison cell, into flashback and then directly into the future scene, whilst still remaining coherent?

Stage four

Ask the groups to create a third scene for their drama based on Image 11:

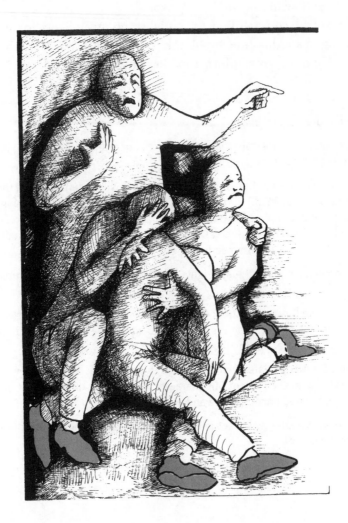

Image 11

- Who might the people in the image be?
- Is one of them Jo, or is Jo 'out of frame'?
- How does this image link to the scenes previously devised?
- The person at the back appears to be saying something. What might it be?

Experiment with ending the scene with different lines of dialogue – for instance:

In the future . . . people will remember this moment . . .

We're sorry . . .

Just you wait . . .

Stage five

The final task for the groups is to revise their work so far, and to devise one last scene which shows the effect that the events depicted have on Jo and his fellow 'Red Shoes'.

Does it have a pessimistic, or optimistic, ending?

How might this situation be resolved?

Was it inevitable that this situation would end in conflict? How could it have been avoided?

Section five – reflection

Stage one

Show images of analogous real-world contexts such as:

- Apartheid-era South Africa.
- Palestine.
- Northern Ireland during 'the Troubles'.
- Segregation in the southern United States of America during the early-mid twentieth century.
- Germany during the Third Reich (1933–45).

Stage two

Ask students to research the historical context of cultural separation/prejudice/ oppression in each case.

How far have the problems depicted in the images and explored through research been resolved, and by what means? How far was violence – or the threat of violence – a factor?

Stage three

Can the students devise a short 'counter-play' which projects the Red Shoe/Black Shoe conflict into the future (5, 10, 100, 1,000 years?) and which shows how things might be *positively* resolved?

The resources for this Unit are available for download at www.routledge.com/ 9780415572064

The case of Lizzie Borden

Lizzie Borden took an axe

Gave her mother forty whacks;

When she saw what she had done

She gave her father forty-one.

Figure 8.1 Lizzie Borden

Thematic content in this unit:	Curriculum connections:
Detective fiction	English, Media Studies
Crime scene investigations	Media studies
Reportage	English, Media Studies
Children's games, stories and rhymes	English, History
Crime and punishment	Citizenship, History
Census information	Citizenship, History
The role of women in society	History, Media Studies, English

Dramatic techniques and keywords in this unit:

Reportage	The Grotesque	Testimony	Flashback
Re-enactment	Elegy	Montage	Choral speech

In this unit students will investigate a 'real crime scenario': the case of Lizzie Borden, accused of brutally murdering her father and stepmother in the USA of the 1890s. They will examine the evidence, including contemporary accounts and photographs, and use this material to create dramatic reconstructions of the possible events of that fateful day. In addition they will consider the mythology that sprung up around the case, and the attitude of society to violent crimes, and those that commit them.[1]

Where this unit connects

Although this unit is based around a detailed exploration of a particular nineteenth century crime, it connects with a number of more contemporary concerns. Lizzie Borden, guilty or not, became perhaps the world's first 'celebrity criminal', with newspapers competing to be first with the latest news on the grim events and repercussions of that hot day in the summer of 1892. As such, students will be able to draw comparisons with the role of the media in more recent criminal *causes célèbres*.

The nineteenth century small-town setting, the horror of the killings and the events of the trial have a melodramatic, almost *grand guignol* element to them, that will appeal to many students in the same way as *Sweeney Todd*, the films of Tim Burton or contemporary vampire fiction. We launch our unit through an exploration of the more grotesque elements of children's nursery rhymes and stories, including Heinrich

The case of Lizzie Borden

Hoffman's *Strewwelpeter* of 1845. This path, of course has already been well trodden by such theatre companies as *The Tiger Lillies*, with their 1998 award-winning musical *Shockheaded Peter*.

The Borden case clearly brings to mind Sir Arthur Conan Doyle's darker *Sherlock Holmes* stories, which were set almost contemporaneously with the events in Massachusetts; even in the absence of the great Baker Street detective, through forensic science, we in the twenty-first century almost *expect* such crimes to be solved. It is likely that if today's technology had been available to the Massachusetts police in 1892 that Lizzie's guilt would have been confirmed – or otherwise – within a very short time. The resulting controversy, and the emergence of Lizzie as an iconic – or *mythic* – character would never have happened. Within the unit, students will also be following in the footsteps of real-life – and fictional – detectives as they examine evidence, and attempt to re-enact the possible course of events.

The fact that Lizzie was a seemingly respectable 32-year-old spinster from a wealthy family – and that she was *female* in a culture where opportunities were limited and expectations strong – was arguably a powerful factor in her eventual acquittal; students will have opportunities to explore something of that claustrophobic small-town environment that was Lizzie's milieu, and, more generally, consider the role of women in nineteenth century society in relation to their own culture and context.

Working in drama: by the end of this unit students will have:

- Created simple performances based on children's rhymes and stories, using narration and choral speaking to emphasize the grotesque.

- Devised and performed a TV news report based on facts known about the crime as they 'unfold'.

- Staged a script excerpt based on the Lizzie Borden episode, and used it as a basis for further devised work.

- Used real crime-scene evidence and testimony to create a dramatic re-enactment of the events surrounding the crime.

- Used drama to speculate about the relationship between Lizzie and the people close to her.

- Experimented with non-naturalistic drama to create a surreal dreamscape.

- Considered the way in which 'myths' are created around famous and infamous people; the role of the media, and the effect of commercialization.

- Created a ritual *elegy* for Lizzie as a means of reflecting on their work.

The Borden case was one of the first murder trials of the era of communication, and the gruesome and macabre details, together with the fact that Lizzie herself was acquitted and the crime unsolved, ensured that the case became a *cause célèbre*, which resonated across the world. Besides huge speculation and controversy, the case also sparked the creation of a large number of books – fiction and non-fiction, films and plays. For those interested in getting their students to research further, there is also a wealth of material – including original source materials, photographs, video clips and transcripts available on the World Wide Web.

The story of Lizzie Borden

Lizzie Borden was born in July 1860, in the small town of Fall River, Massachusetts. Lizzie's mother had died when Lizzie was less than three years old, and her father, Andrew Borden, had remarried; Lizzie also had a sister, Emma, who was nine years her senior. A third sister died whilst still a baby.

Lizzie's stepmother, Abby Durfee Gray, married Andrew Borden in 1865, and for a time the four of them lived an uneventful life in the town. The family were reasonably wealthy, although the house had few modern conveniences and no running water. The father's stinginess apparently caused some conflicts; there were arguments about money, and in early July 1892, Lizzie and Emma were sent away for some time to stay with friends, returning some weeks later.

On 4 August, the 70-year-old Andrew Borden returned from a trip to town and lay down on a couch in the sitting room. Emma, Lizzie's elder sister, was away visiting relations. The house was quiet.

After a busy morning, the maid, Bridget Sullivan, was taking a nap in an attic bedroom; at about 11.15, she was awakened by Lizzie, who shouted urgently to her to come downstairs. In the sitting room, Andrew Borden lay dead, having been bludgeoned savagely about the face and head with a sharp instrument – probably an axe. Bridget was sent for help, the local doctor was called, and the dead body of 65-year-old Abby Borden was found in a bedroom, who had died in a similar way.

A police investigation was launched and, although there were other suspects (including Bridget Sullivan the maid, and Andrew Borden's brother-in-law, John Morse, who was staying with the family at the time, but had a strong alibi), after a week of gathering evidence Lizzie was accused of the murders. Her trial began in June 1893 and lasted 17 days. Lizzie herself never testified, preferring to let her expensive lawyers speak for her. Her story was that she was planning a fishing expedition and had been searching for fishing equipment in the house's barn at the time of the murders, and that she was completely innocent.

Due to the circumstantial evidence the jury could not come to a firm conclusion as to Lizzie's guilt, and she was acquitted of the murders on 20 June 1893.

Section one – children's games

Stage one

As an introduction to the unit, ask the students to consider children's stories or rhymes with which they are familiar that have cruel or grotesque endings. In the words of Iona

The case of Lizzie Borden

and Peter Opie,[2] nursery rhymes, *are fragments of ballads or of folk songs, remnants of ancient custom and ritual and may hold the last echoes of long-forgotten evil.*

Examples might be *Little Red Riding Hood,* with grandma being eaten by the wolf, *The Three Little Pigs,* killing the wolf in a pot of boiling water, or nursery rhymes like these:

> *Goosey Goosey Gander, where shall I wander,*
> *Upstairs, downstairs and in my lady's chamber.*
> *There I met an old man who wouldn't say his prayers,*
> *I took him by the left leg and threw him down the stairs.*

> *Three blind mice*
> *Three blind mice,*
> *See how they run!*
> *They all ran after the farmer's wife,*
> *Who cut off their tails with a carving knife.*
> *Did you ever see such a thing in your life,*
> *As three blind mice?*

> *Rock-a-bye baby, in the tree top,*
> *When the wind blows, the cradle will rock.*
> *When the bough breaks, the cradle will fall,*
> *And down will come baby, cradle and all.*

> *Solomon Grundy,*
> *Born on Monday,*
> *Christened on Tuesday,*
> *Married on Wednesday,*
> *Took ill on Thursday,*
> *Worse on Friday,*
> *Died on Saturday,*
> *Buried on Sunday,*
> *This is the end of Solomon Grundy.*

Some students may also be familiar with early children's stories with a grotesque element that aim to teach a moral lesson such as Heinrich Hoffman's *Strewwelpeter* of 1845[3]:

One day Mamma said 'Conrad dear,
I must go out and leave you here.
But mind now, Conrad, what I say,
Don't suck your thumb while I'm away.
The great tall tailor always comes
To little boys who suck their thumbs;
And ere they dream what he's about,
He takes his great sharp scissors out,
And cuts their thumbs clean off and then,
You know, they never grow again.'
Mamma had scarcely turned her back,
The thumb was in, Alack! Alack!
The door flew open, in he ran,
The great, long, red-legged scissor-man.
Oh! children, see! the tailor's come
And caught out little Suck-a-Thumb.
Snip! Snap! Snip! the scissors go;
And Conrad cries out 'Oh! Oh! Oh!'
Snip! Snap! Snip! They go so fast,
That both his thumbs are off at last.
Mamma comes home: there Conrad stands,
And looks quite sad, and shows his hands;
'Ah!' said Mamma, 'I knew he'd come
To naughty little Suck-a-Thumb.'

Figure 8.2 'Suck-a-thumb'

The case of Lizzie Borden

In groups of three to five ask the students to compose a series of still images to recreate key moments in their chosen fairytale or nursery rhyme, making sure that they focus on the cruel, violent or dark elements. More able students could work on excerpts from the *Strewwelpeter* text.

To enhance the presentation of the tableaux ask the groups to add narration, chanting or choral speaking. More able students could link the tableaux to create a stylized movement sequence. Select one group to work on the Lizzie Borden rhyme:

> *Lizzie Borden took an axe*
> *Gave her mother forty whacks;*
> *When she saw what she had done*
> *She gave her father forty-one.*

Ensure that this group performs last in the sequence.

Share and evaluate the work:

- How effective were the performances?

- How well did groups capture the dark, violent elements of the stories and rhymes?

- Why might rhymes and stories intended for children have violent, bloodthirsty elements?

- Focusing on the final piece based on the Borden rhyme, are the groups familiar with the story of Lizzie Borden? What do they know of her?

Section two – reportage

Stage one

Figure 8.3 Sketches of the bodies of Lizzie's stepmother, Abby Borden and father, Andrew J. Borden

The basic facts

- The murders took place on 4 August 1892, at about 11am.

- The town was called Falls River, in America.

- Lizzie's stepmother, Abby Borden, and father, Andrew J. Borden, were murdered in the family home. They had been hacked about the face and head in a brutal attack.

- The murder weapon was a sharp instrument, probably an axe.

- An axe was found at the scene, it had a broken handle.

- Lizzie and the family maid, Bridget Sullivan, were at home at the time.

- The Borden family were rich and owned a lot of businesses in the town.

Gather the group and tell them the outline story of Lizzie Borden and the events surrounding the day of the murders.

In groups of four or five, using the 'basic facts' sheet and the crime scene sketches, ask the students to reconstruct a television news report from the scene of the crime, focusing on the horror of the event, its effect on a small community and the tension and suspense surrounding the murders. Each group might include:

- Studio and 'location' footage.

- Witness interviews.

- A police statement.

- A request for members of the public to come forward with evidence.

Share the presentations, and encourage the group to reflect on their work.

How well did the reports capture the sense of a shocked community coming to terms with a brutal crime?

Inform the group that Lizzie was arrested and put on trial for the crimes – and that we will be investigating these events later. For now, the focus will turn to Lizzie's childhood, to see if there might be clues about her state of mind, personality, and – assuming that she was guilty – to investigate what might turn a privileged young woman into someone who would brutally murder her own parents?

Section three – exploring Lizzie's childhood

Stage one

How do children behave when there are no adults around?

What do they talk about?

In groups of two or three, prepare a short scene showing Lizzie, as a child, talking with other children in the school playground. Ask for suggestions for topics of conversation:

The case of Lizzie Borden

- *What are you going to be when you grow up?*
- *What happens to people when they die?*
- *What should happen to bad people?*

Ask the groups to pinpoint any significant point in the drama (*marking the moment*[4]) when something is revealed about Lizzie and her world. Share the scenes and ask the group to reflect on what is potentially significant – for what it might reveal about Lizzie's situation or state of mind – in each case.

Stage two

Distribute the following script excerpt. In groups of four to seven (there are seven characters in the script as written but parts can easily be doubled) ask the students to stage the script.

A Memory of Lizzie

from *Sepia and Song* by David Foxton

Auditorium lights fade down slowly: we hear children's voices singing – if it is a proscenium stage they are still behind the main curtain, if open stage then the cast enter, singing, to their positions.

Oranges and lemons

Say the bells of St. Clements

You owe me five farthings

Say the bells of St. Martins.

When will you pay me?

Say the bells of Old Bailey.

When I grow rich

Say the bells of Shoreditch.

When will that be?

Say the bells of Stepney.

I'm sure I don't know

Says the great bell of Bow.

Here comes a candle

To light you to bed

And here comes a chopper to chop off your head

Chop

    Chop

        Chop

            CHOP

During the song the main curtain opens, or the lights come up if on an open stage, showing figures in silhouette playing the game of 'Oranges and Lemons' in a small American schoolyard – Massachusetts in about 1871/2.

Lizzie Borden is caught on the fourth chop. She is normally very sure of herself, but now she screams and a spotlight comes up on Lizzie held between two other children, Ann and Barbara; all are frozen except Lizzie.

Lizzie:	My full name is Lizzie Andrew Borden and I am 32 years of age. I have always lived in Fall River. My mother died when I was two. My father married my stepmother when I was five. The day they were killed I had on a blue dress. I went to school in Fall River . . . twenty years ago.
Lizzie *(Breaking away)*:	Let me go . . . Let me go . . . Why've you caught me? Let me go . . .
Ann:	It's only a game, Lizzie.
Barbara:	An' you was caught fair and square.
Lizzie:	No I wasn't, you made it be me . . . You all wanted it to be me that was caught.
Barbara:	Come on Lizzie – y'know that's not so.
Lizzie:	It is! It is! It's always me that ends up getting caught – never anyone else. I ain't gonna play any more.

(She exits stage left. The others disperse around the 'playground' area and pick up items for other games; e.g. a ball, a hoop, a whip and top.)

Barbara:	What's the matter with her now?
Christy:	Leave her be – she'll come round.
Ann:	Never plays fair . . .
Dorothy:	Can't take a joke – never could.
Eliza:	Thinks too much of herself.
Dorothy:	Just 'cos she's a Borden – thinks she owns the whole place.
Frances:	Thinks she owns the whole world.
Dorothy:	Lizzie Borden can't take a joke.

The case of Lizzie Borden

Present the various versions of the scene. What do the scenes suggest about Lizzie and her family, and how others regard them in the town?

Ask the class to focus on the way that Lizzie is portrayed as 'different' in the scene and the significance of the final six lines of the excerpt.

Stage three

Working in groups of four or five, ask the students to develop the scripted scene further – so that we learn more about the rumours and gossip spread around the town. What might be the 'myth' about her family – what makes them different?

Some suggestions:

- The children plan their 'revenge' on Lizzie for 'owning the whole world'.

- The children play a joke on Lizzie, thus pointing to the sinister implication of the final line of the excerpt.

- We see a parallel scene to the first, but this time played out by the children's parents who behave in a similar – but *adult* – way to their children.

Share the scenes. Encourage reflection: as *playwrights*, what do the students feel 'works best' in these scenes, and why?

Stage four

In pairs, ask the students to consider the information given in the 1880 Census (12 years previous to the murders) about the Borden household:

Table 8.1 References to the Borden family in 1880 Census

Name	Gender	Age	Place in Household	Marital Status	Occupation	Place of Origin
Borden, Andrew J.	M	57	Head	M	Retired Merchant	MA
Borden, Abby D.	F	52	Wife	M	Keeping House	MA
Borden, Emma L.	F	29	Daughter	S	At Home	MA
Borden, Lizzie A.	F	19	Daughter	S	At Home	MA
Green, Mary	F	35	Servant	S	Servant	Ireland

What can be learnt about the Borden household from this information? What might be *inferred* from the Census data?

Does this add anything that might be significant about the way that the family lived? For instance, does the fact that they had a live-in servant, whilst the two daughters were not employed, suggest anything about their lifestyle?

In reality, the Bordens were a wealthy family, but Lizzie's father, Andrew Borden, was notoriously mean, and appeared unconcerned about his daughters' prospects – despite the fact that they were both unmarried and had no independent means of support. Shortly before the time of the murders there had been some conflict in the family concerning property and money, which had resulted in the two sisters being sent away on 'holiday'.

In one bizarre incident Lizzie found that her father had used an axe to chop the heads off the pigeons she kept in the family barn, on the grounds that the birds were attracting the unwanted attention of local children.

In another, the entire household had become ill with food poisoning as a result of Andrew Borden purchasing cheap meat, and continually reheating it to serve up over several days.

In groups of five, ask the class to improvise a scene, which takes place in the weeks before the murder, with all members of the household present – perhaps a mealtime – where tensions between the members of the household become apparent.

Within the scene, ask the groups to create – in *flashback*[5] – a moment from Lizzie's life when she is isolated or under stress. Stop the drama at the appropriate time and ask the student portraying Lizzie to speak Lizzie's thoughts at that particular moment.

Reflect on the work. Do the dramas give any insight into the possible relationships within the family?

Section four – giving witness

Figure 8.4 Crime scene photographs
Source: http://law2.umkc.edu/faculty/projects/ftrials/LizzieBorden/andrewbody.jpg and http://law2.umkc.edu/faculty/projects/ftrials/LizzieBorden/abbybody.jpg

The case of Lizzie Borden

Figure 8.4 Continued

Reports on the finding of the bodies:

> *Abby had apparently been hacked by someone who stood astride the body after the first blow (probably the one on the nape of the neck) had felled her. Her blood had spurted forward and not high or wide; there was none on the bedspread just beside her, and of the wall in front of her head only the skirting board was stained.*

> *Borden's head was bent slightly to the right, but his face was almost unrecognizable as human; one eye had been cut in half and protruded in a ghastly manner, his nose had been severed, and there were eleven distinct cuts within a relatively small area extending from the eye and nose to the ears. Fresh blood was still seeping from the wounds, which were so severe that the first of the eleven blows must have killed him.*

Stage one

Working in groups of four or five ask students to create the *testimony* of one of the people who – as part of the police investigation – may have been asked for their account of the events of that day:

- Bridget Sullivan, the family's maidservant.
- Lizzie Borden herself.
- A by-passer who happened to be in the vicinity at the time.

- The neighbour who was first on the scene.
- The family doctor who first investigated the bodies.

If necessary, students can research their account from one of the many websites giving background to the case.

> **Testimony**: a formal written or spoken statement, especially one given in a court of law.

Once the groups have created their accounts, form different groups of 4 or 5 made up of students who can represent each of the different witnesses' testimonies. In their new groups, ask students to consider the accounts they have, and re-enact, as a short piece of drama, the events of 4 August 1892.

- Was Lizzie guilty of the crimes, or not? If not, who might have committed them?
- Can their dramas present a coherent account of the events of the day based on the evidence available?

A suitable form for this depiction of events may be *directed re-enactment*.

In this way of working, one of the performers becomes a director/narrator, who is able to freeze the action at significant points, and, using direct address to the audience, comment on the characters and events. The director/narrator is able to take a 'stance' on the events being enacted, and does not necessarily have to be disinterested; in this case, as a number of characters' narratives may intersect in a complex way, the technique should enable a clear exposition of the events on the morning of the murder as the students piece them together from their previously improvised testimony.

Stage two – missing evidence

In actual fact, Lizzie was acquitted of the murders, and no one was ever found guilty of the crimes. This was hugely controversial at the time, and to this day, conjecture – as to the real culprit, and their motivation for the crimes – is still rife.

One of the reasons why the verdict was so controversial is that for various reasons important evidence was not collected, not considered or deemed insignificant at the trial:

The case of Lizzie Borden

Missing evidence 1

The hatchet

At the time of the police investigation of the murders, a small hatchet was found in the basement of the house. This hatchet was assumed to be the weapon that had been used to murder John Morse and Abby Borden. The handle of the hatchet had been broken off and was missing, and at the trial it was inferred that Lizzie had broken the handle off because it was smeared with the blood of her victims.

The police presented contradictory accounts, with one officer claiming that the missing handle was lying next to the hatchet when it was found, though the handle was never presented as evidence. The hatchet blade was never tested for fingerprints, as at the time the Fall River police did not have much faith in the 'new' technology of forensic science.

Missing evidence 2

Lizzie's clothes

Despite the violence of the attack, no bloodstained clothing was found at the house or presented as evidence, and this was a key factor in the trial, as it planted enough doubt in the minds of the jury to acquit Lizzie.

Three days after the trial Lizzie was observed tearing up and burning a blue dress in the furnace in the kitchen of the house. She claimed that she had brushed against a freshly painted fence and this 'brown paint' had stained the dress.

Missing evidence 3

Prussic acid

On the day before the murders Lizzie had attempted to buy prussic acid – cyanide poison – from a local pharmacist. She claimed that she needed the prussic acid to clean a stained sealskin cape. The pharmacist, a man named Eli Bence, refused to sell her the poison.

This evidence was ruled inadmissible at the trial, and the jury was not allowed to consider it.

Present the groups with the 'missing evidence'. Does this add anything to their understanding of the events of the day of the murders? Does it change their minds as to Lizzie's guilt?

Can they re-work their re-enactments to take account of the new evidence?

Section five – after the trial

Stage one – Lizzie and her sister

> Although Lizzie was found not guilty of the murders, the people of the town, convinced of her guilt, ostracized her. Despite this, she did continue to live out her life in Fall River.
>
> After the trial Lizzie changed her name to Lizbeth, and she and her sister Emma bought a large, well-appointed house in an up-market area of Fall River, and they lived there together for twelve years. In 1905, Emma and Lizzie fell out, and Emma moved out of the house.
>
> When Lizzie Borden died of pneumonia in 1927, she left an estate worth over $250,000. She owned a large house and several office buildings, had live-in maids, a chauffeur, two cars, and extensive investments.
>
> Lizzie left her wealth to those members of her family and friends who had stood by her. She did not leave her sister, Emma, anything in her will, supposedly because Emma had already received her share of her father's estate. Lizzie did, however, leave $30,000 to the local animal protection league. (Interestingly enough, there is a story – perhaps an urban legend – that some years before the murders Lizzie killed one of her stepmother's cats in the house's cellar. According to the story, she killed it by beheading it with an axe.)

In pairs, ask the students to create a short scene from Lizzie's life with her sister. In the scene, focus the work on a moment that might help the group to understand the sisters' relationship – and, in particular, the episode of the will.

Encourage the students to try to capture the moment when the two sisters' relationship – in a claustrophobic small town full of people who suspect and despise you – started to go wrong.

Share the work.

Set design

Based on the work so far, design the set for the first part of David Foxton's play about Lizzie Borden, *A Memory of Lizzie* (see stage two, above).

Will the set attempt to recreate the town/house and environs realistically, or be more symbolic?

What are the key elements of the set? How might you suggest the threat of violence to come later, which is pre-figured by the *Oranges and Lemons* sequence?

It may be useful to do some research in order to get ideas: an Internet image search for 'set design' will provide lots of examples to study.

Task: produce sketches or a simple model of your design. Be prepared to talk about your ideas in class.

Section six – Lizzie's nightmare

Stage one

In the years following the crimes, perhaps only Lizzie herself really knew the truth about her guilt or innocence. Ask the students to imagine a time when Lizzie is finally alone in the house on her own; her sister has left. One night, Lizzie has a nightmare about the events of her life, her childhood, her relationships.

In groups of four to six, ask the students to create Lizzie's nightmare using the following prompts to structure their performances:

1 Begin the drama with Lizzie falling asleep; she must then be *in* the nightmare.

2 Choose three of the following to include in the nightmare sequence:

- the cat incident – described above;
- gossiping neighbours;
- her dead parents haunting her;
- children in the playground teasing her for being 'different';
- a scary story her stepmother told her when she was little;
- the grotesque children's rhymes and stories explored in Section 1.

3 Finish the drama with a tableau, held at a moment of high tension, which shows something *really* bad about to happen!

Ask the students to suggest drama techniques that might recreate the surreal, non-linear form of a dream or nightmare.

For instance, in order to help students capture the desired atmosphere, you might suggest that although Lizzie *sees* all of these things in her dream, she can hear music rather than voices in some episodes: ask the students to select appropriate music to enhance the atmosphere and mood of their work.

Share the work:

- How effectively did the pieces capture the essence of a dream or nightmare?
- What techniques worked best and why?
- What insight do the pieces give us into Lizzie's possible state of mind as she lives alone with her secrets?

Dream sequences

Although there are a number of clichés to be avoided in assisting students to create dream sequences,[6] sequences of this kind are a useful means of introducing inexperienced students to non-naturalistic, more abstract or physical forms of drama.

Techniques that might be fruitfully employed in dream sequences include choral speaking, slow motion, repetitive dialogue or movement, dance and figurative mime; students will be keen to contribute their own suggestions.

Work of this kind can be substantially enhanced through the use of atmospheric music and theatre technology; lighting, projections – even smoke!

Section seven – Lizzie Borden: the myth

Stage one

Lizzie, of course, lives on in the children's rhyme, but she has also entered 'popular culture' in other ways, with a multitude of websites, books, plays, films, opera and even a board game based on her life!

The house where the murder took place, 92 Second Street, Fall River, has now been turned into *The Lizzie Borden Bed and Breakfast*, complete with 'ghost cams' and a gift shop.

Present to the group some of the *Lizzie Borden* items available for sale on the World Wide Web[7]:

Brick dust

Be the first of your friends to own a little piece of Lizzie Borden history!

This is authentic brick dust collected from the decaying bricks in the said to be haunted basement of the Borden home at 92 Second Street.

Lizzie Borden hatchet earrings

Silver tone pierced earrings with dangling hatchets.

Looking sharp!

Lizzie Borden head knocker (bobble head).

Can it be more fun? Hand painted collectable.

Death certificate included on box.

Approx 8 inches tall.

What is the students' reaction to the commercialization of the Lizzie Borden 'myth'?

Could they invent their own 'Lizzie' merchandise, and make a pitch to the rest of the class as in the TV programme, *Dragon's Den*?

The case of Lizzie Borden

Stage two

As a final exercise, ask students to think of a phrase, line of dialogue or statement that has stayed with them as they have explored *The Case of Lizzie Borden*.

In masking tape, draw the outline of a body on the floor, lower the lights, and gather the students around. Ask each student in turn to speak his or her 'memorable phrase as a kind of *elegy* for this enigmatic woman. This might take some choreographing. Encourage experimentation with dynamics and delivery to find an effective mood for the montage of voices. Finish with a whispered ensemble rendition of Lizzie's rhyme:

> *Lizzie Borden took an axe*
>
> *Gave her mother forty whacks*
>
> *When she saw what she had done*
>
> *She gave her father forty-one.*

Celebrity criminals

Research other high-profile female criminals.[8]

Suggestions might include:

- Ruth Ellis.

- Myra Hindley.

- Beverley Allitt.

Why does society – and in particular, the media – find them so fascinating?

Do they get treated in the same way as men by the media, judicial system, etc?

In the cases you researched, are there any parallels with the case of Lizzie Borden? What are the key similarities and differences?

If the case of Lizzie Borden happened in contemporary society what do you think would be the likely outcome?

Task: write a newspaper account of *The Case of Lizzie Borden* as though it had only happened last week.

Stage three – reflections on Lizzie Borden

Ask the students to reflect on the project as a whole. How far has it raised their awareness of the following key questions/issues?

- Are murderers *born*, or *raised*?

- How much are students aware of the place of women in nineteenth century society? How far did the fact that Lizzie was a young woman from a respectable family play a part in her acquittal?

- Can they think of other, more recent cases, where high-profile crimes – or criminals – have become *causes célèbres* and entered popular culture and myth?

- How far is using drama in this way – to dramatize or *fictionalize* real events – a valid means of exploring history? Are there any dangers in such an approach?

The resources for this Unit are available for download at www.routledge.com/9780415572064

Kindertransport

Thematic content in this unit:	Curriculum connections:
Refugees and asylum seekers	History, PSHE, Geography
Family and identity	PSHE, English
Keepsakes and mementos	PSHE, History
Germany and National Socialism	History, Citizenship

Dramatic techniques and keywords in this unit:

Split stage	Naturalism	Character development
Hot-seating	Motivation	Given circumstances
Group devising	Stylization	Elegy

In this unit students have the opportunity to explore a poignant moment in European history – the evacuation of thousands of Jewish children from Nazi Germany on the verge of the Second World War – The *Kindertransport*.

Where this unit connects

There are a number of times in history where large movements of people occur, often suddenly and without warning. This unit is an attempt to examine a very specific moment from our past, where 10,000 children became 'displaced people', leaving behind their homes and parents – many of whom would themselves later become displaced people and refugees.

The surviving children of the *Kindertransport* are often referred to as *Kind*.

The political and social landscape in Europe leading up to the Second World War was volatile and complex, and as such there is a considerable amount of contextual material included in the unit. As they work through the drama activities in the unit we hope that students will understand a little of the bravery and sacrifice – and at times desperation – of those involved in the *Kindertransport*. There is much about the *Kindertransport* that we have not been able to detail, for instance, Sir Nicholas Winton's rescue of 669 mainly Jewish children from the former Czechoslovakia. We hope that by accessing some of the rich material available from websites like **The Weiner Library, National Archives** and **Imperial War Museum**, students can develop their understanding of these events further.

Within the curriculum the unit clearly connects with History and Citizenship, particularly in the areas of cultural diversity and identity, and offers an avenue into further exploration of the Holocaust.

A striking metaphor and possible starting point for this exploration could be taken from Frank Meisler's sculpture, *Trains to Life, Trains to Death,* in Friedrichstrasse Railway Station, Berlin. The brass sculpture depicts a pair of children embarking on their *Kindertransport* journey to freedom, while behind them, and facing the other way, another group of children embark on their journey to the death camps.

Working in drama: by the end of this unit students will have:

- Used a range of drama techniques to explore sensitive and emotive material.

- Worked on script excerpts written by a professional playwright on the same topic to draw comparisons with their own devised work.

- Explored some of the ideas of Stanislavski and applied them to building characters in naturalistic drama.

- Worked on an extended ensemble dramatic sequence based on structured resource sheets.

- Created a poetic *elegy* as a means of reflecting on the topic.

Section one

Stage one

Gather the students into a circle and explain that this drama project starts with a simple story. Ask for three volunteers and place them in the middle of the circle. Tell them that as you read through the brief narrative, you want them to create a simple still image or a simple piece of mimed action to illustrate your words. Tell them you will indicate which role they are acting out and when to change their image or actions. Explain you might want them to repeat some of the words you are narrating. Use this simple script to re-tell the story with the volunteers creating images and voicing some of the dialogue with your prompts.

Kindertransport

*Once upon a time there was a **mother** and **father** who sent their beloved **son** and **daughter** away.*

The children had not been naughty or bad at school.
The children were not the cause of the problem the family faced.

The father lied and said, 'It is only for a short time.'
The mother lied and said that they would be re-united soon.

The mother took her children's hands in hers.

She said, 'In England, they will look after you.'
She said, 'In England, there are people like us and you will be treated well.'
She said, 'When the war is over, we will come and bring you home.'

The children asked, 'Who will we live with?'
The children asked, 'When will we be able to come home?'
The children asked, 'Why can't you come too?'

The mother listened but did not answer. Instead, she quietly turned away and began packing one little brown suitcase for the brother and sister. In each one she put a keepsake, a reminder of who they were and where they had come from.

The father told the children, 'These things will help you remember us. These things will remind you that you are loved.'

At the train station, the family hurriedly said their goodbyes. The children climbed aboard the train and joined the others. The carriage windows would not open so they waved through the glass as the train pulled away.

This was the last time the children would ever see their parents.

Ask the students to hold their final still image and open a group discussion by asking the audience what they think the story might be about. When do they think the story is set? What reasons might there be for parents to send away their children to another country? What might have happened to the parents or the children so that they never meet again? What is the longest journey they have ever taken alone?

Tell the students that, as the drama unfolds, they will learn more of what happens to the children in the story.

Stage two

Arrange the students into groups of four or five. Explain that the next part of the work will be about exploring *families, memories* and *identity.*

Ask the students to consider how important they think childhood memories might be in shaping the people they are today.

Next, ask the class to think about their own past and identify a story from their childhood that might get told and re-told at family gatherings. It is worth explaining that as these stories will be shared they should only present memories that are not private, embarrassing or too personally exposing. The tone of this work should be light and affirmative, so try and encourage your students to think of events that represent a happy or positive time.

After the groups have had a short time to swap their stories, explain that they need to choose one story that they will focus on for the next task. Inform them that they are going to create a family photograph album, and that each group is going to contribute one still image to the album. Explain that as each 'photograph' is 'labelled' in the album, they need to provide a caption for their image. Allow time for groups to create their still image and rehearse how they are going to integrate their spoken caption or title – which could be spoken by one member of the group, as a chorus in unison, or broken up and shared between different group members.

After five minutes, stop the work in progress and explain the next part of the work. Tell the groups that they now have a choice; they can create one minute of dramatic action leading up to the moment the photograph was taken, or one minute of action immediately following the photograph. In this way, groups will either start or finish their drama with a still image and caption.

Allow the groups time to shape their drama before arranging them in a circle around the room. Explain that each group will perform in turn as if they were turning the pages of a photograph album.

Share the work and lead a discussion:

Figure 9.1 Young refugee from Nazi Germany
Source: http://www.movinghere.org.uk/galleries/roots/intro/migration/parliament5.htm

Kindertransport

- Which of the groups best captured the idea of childhood and family life?

- Do the students recognize a shared experience of childhood?

- Do any of the stories have similarities to each other – or to the students' own real life experiences?

- How important are memories and childhood experiences in shaping the people we grow up to become?

Stage two

Tell the students that there is one more image that they need to see. Explain that in this photograph album the photographs end abruptly with this final entry. Project or hand out the image of a girl, pensively clutching her doll and holding her bag. Explain to the class that she is on board a ship that sailed from Holland to England in December 1938.

Ask the students what might be significant about the date. It is, of course, a few months before the start of the Second World War. Why would a young girl be making a journey apparently by herself, and why might she be coming to England?

Write or project the word *Kindertransport* on the board and tell the group that this is the word that describes the rescue of thousands of children who were at risk from the policies of Hitler's National Socialist (Nazi) government. The majority of the *Kindertransport* children came from Jewish families in Germany, Austria and the former Czechoslovakia. In the nine months leading up to the start of the war, around 10,000 children were given safe passage to travel to Great Britain to be placed with host families, boarding schools and care homes. The *Kind*, as they are known, could not have realized that most of their parents and family, left behind in Nazi Europe, would eventually become victims of the Holocaust. Once war was declared in 1939, the *Kindertransport* was stopped.

Hand out the resource sheet that will help give their work its proper historical context. The resource sheet charts the rise of National Socialism and the anti-Jewish sentiments that fuelled the Holocaust, and identifies just how difficult life became for Jewish people once Hitler had been appointed Chancellor in January 1933.

Resource sheet – Hitler and anti-semitism

In January 1933 Adolph Hitler was appointed Chancellor, and over the next seven years, National Socialism grew in Germany. Germany, like other countries around the world, had been suffering economically and Hitler and his leaders wanted to restore Germany back to a position of strength. Hitler felt particularly angry over the loss of land and power that countries like Great Britain had imposed as a punishment for Germany's role in starting the First World War.

There were many people that Hitler blamed for Germany's problems, but it was the German Jewish population that bore the brunt of his hatred. Before Hitler's rise to power, German Jews were well integrated into the country's population and many had become successful in their chosen fields – Jewish people made up 11 per cent of the doctors and 16 per cent of the lawyers in Germany. There were feelings of jealousy and anger at the success of many Jewish businesses.

Hitler promoted the idea that true Germans were a race of superior beings and that Jewish people were polluting the pure blood lines of Aryans and stopping Germany from achieving its potential and destiny of ruling the world.

Jewish people were blamed for infiltrating banks and businesses and robbing Germany of its wealth as well as encouraging people to believe in equality, when Hitler's ideal world was one based on superiority and domination as a natural order.

Using relentless propaganda and unfair laws that took away the rights and freedom of Jewish people, the hatred and persecution of any non-Aryan grew in Germany in the years leading up to the Second World War.

Jewish businesses and shops were marked with a painted Star of David or the word *Juden* on their windows. Later, Jewish owned businesses had to be given away completely to Germans. From 1935 Jewish people lost the right to be German citizens and the right to vote in elections. Marriages between Jews and non-Jews were banned, identity cards had to be carried and names changed to include *Israel* for men and *Sarah* for women.

Being a Jewish child under the Nazis meant succumbing to a number of laws and being humiliated and intimidated on a daily basis. Theatres, parks and other public spaces became out of bounds. At school, new compulsory lessons were introduced, designed to propagate the Nazi belief in the inferiority of Jews.

Jewish children would be separated from their German classmates or made to stand at the front while the teacher explained why Jews were the 'enemy of the people'. Eventually Jewish children had to attend separate schools, until even those schools were closed down.

During this time, desperate Jewish families looked for an escape to safer and more sympathetic countries. However, many governments were reluctant to open their doors to Jewish refugees. It took an outrageous act of chaos and violence in Germany on 9 and 10 November 1938, that made the British Government change its mind. *Kristallnacht* – 'The Night of Broken Glass' – saw the organized destruction and looting of hundreds of synagogues and thousands of houses and Jewish businesses. Ninety-one people were murdered, countless people were beaten and intimidated and 26,000 Jewish men were rounded up and transported to concentration camps.

The events of that night were widely reported to a shocked world and soon after the *Kindertransport* began ferrying children out of danger to England. As Europe was on

Kindertransport

the verge of war, speed and urgency were crucial in order to save as many children as possible. Various charities and individuals worked together to find host families in Great Britain and the required £50 bond per child. The Home Office waived the need for passports and visas and teams of volunteers travelled to Germany, Austria and the former Czechoslovakia to select the children. News spread quickly by word of mouth and desperate families began queuing up to secure a place for their children on the transport.

It was I who heard about the transport! I met a school friend who told me that he was going to England . . . and I asked him 'How so?' and he told me that children were being recruited at the Hotel Metropole . . . and I turned around and ran to join the queue of children. My parents had to sign documents later . . . It's just as well I did turn around and ran quickly because 360 children were registered that day and I was child 359![1]

Because of the amount of children wanting a place, there was a selection process with preference given to orphans or children whose parents had been deported. Forms had to be filled in, photographs taken and files returned to London.

Successful families would be informed and given the date of their transport, often with only a few days' notice. They would be told to take the children to a train station to catch a specially scheduled train. Under the watchful eyes of the Gestapo and police, parents would say a hasty goodbye. Children would be allowed to take one suitcase of clothes, which they had to be able to carry themselves. No valuables or cash were allowed and the Gestapo often searched their cases. Jewish adults, who were ordered to return after each trip, accompanied the children. If these chaperones tried to escape themselves, all further transports would be cancelled.

The first transport left Berlin on 1 December 1938. During the first few months, children would arrive in England twice weekly, though as momentum grew this increased to daily arrivals during the summer of 1939. Around 10,000 children were transported to England; of those the majority were Jewish, but there were other refugees from countries like Poland and the former Czechoslovakia. The final transport left two days before the start of the war.

Once the students have had a chance to work with the resource sheet, lead a discussion based on the following:

- Why do you think some Jewish families did not leave Germany when the situation began to get difficult for them?
- What feelings do you think parents would have had before deciding to enroll their children on the *Kindertransport*?
- How do you think the parents might have explained the *Kindertransport* to their children? Do you think they told them the truth?

Stage three

Ask the students to form groups of four and label themselves A, B, C and D.
    Give the students the following information to clarify their roles:

A and B, you are the Jewish parents of C and D. It is December 1938 and life has been extremely challenging for your family over the last few years. You have heard of the Kindertransport and how it aims to re-settle children in England and away from persecution in Germany. Tomorrow morning you have the opportunity to enroll your children at the town hall. Your drama is going to show the thoughts and feelings these parents might have about the decision they are to make.

You have to speak quietly because your children are next door!

C and D, you are the children of A and B. Decide on your character's age; avoid being younger than seven and make sure that one of you is a few years older than the other. You have heard rumours about children being sent away to another country, and wonder if it might happen to you: you don't know how long for and if your parents can come too. Discuss the rumours you have heard and your feelings about having to leave your home.

You have to speak quietly because your parents are next door!

Explain that the drama should be as 'naturalistic' as possible and in this way they are attempting to capture believable and realistic language, movement and character. Remind the group that this work is based on real events that affected thousands of people and, as such, should be treated with respect.

Tell the group that they will have to think about arranging the performance space carefully to show that the parents and children are separated and in different rooms. This is sometimes called *split-stage* and the challenge is creating drama that cuts from one side to the other smoothly and effectively. In preparation, the pairs will have to shape individual conversations and then find a way of ensuring the focus is on one side of the stage only.

In order to help the audience focus, ask the pairs to consider the use of still image for one side when the other is 'performing'. Using a shared or repeated word or phrase to end the parents' conversation and then start the children's is also theatrically effective. Alternatively, one side can mime their conversation and simplify their actions as the other side voice their lines. If you have access to technical equipment, students can enhance the split-stage staging by using lighting. Explain that that their performance should aim to cut back and forth a number of times.

Allow 20 minutes for the groups to shape their drama before assigning a performance space and sharing the work in turn. Evaluate the work, focusing on the emotive content of the drama and how effectively feelings were communicated.

Places of origin

This exercise is about exploring the locations of the cities that the children of the *Kindertransport* were evacuated from. You will need access to a map of Europe or an atlas. The larger the scale of the map, the easier your task will be.

Task: using the list of cities below, identify each of them on the map using a pin or marker.

Berlin,	Bremen,	Breslau,	Cologne,	Danzig,	Düsseldorf,
Frankfurt am Main,		Hamburg,	Hanover,	Leipzig,	Mannheim,
Munich,	Nuremberg,	Stuttgart,	Prague,	Vienna.	

Now identify on your map where the Hook of Holland is. From here, the children departed to England on ferries to Harwich. From there, many of the children travelled on trains to meet their host families and carers at Liverpool Street Station in London.

Many of the Jewish children felt a great sense of relief as they crossed the border into the Netherlands, and many recalled the kindness of the volunteers meeting them, helping them on their long journey to England. During the war, the Netherlands was occupied by the Germans, and the Dutch Jewish population faced the same fate as their neighbours at the hands of the Nazis.

Famously, one Jewish family living in Amsterdam went into hiding in a secret annex of an office building in 1942. Their family name was Frank and the 13-year-old Anne began recording their two years of hiding in a diary she had been given for her birthday. In August 1944, however, the Franks were betrayed and captured. The family members were split up and sent to concentration camps. Only Otto Frank, Anne's father, survived. He returned to Amsterdam, and in 1947, Anne's diary was published.

Do some research and find out more about Anne Frank, her diary and her family. Find out why she has become such an important figure by visiting the official Anne Frank Museum website.[2]

Finally, why not become one of the millions of people who have read her famous diary?

Stage four

The next section of the work introduces a play called *Kindertransport* by Diane Samuels.[3]

Nine-year-old Eva is sent by her parents from Germany, eventually ending up in Manchester, being looked after by a woman called Lil Miller. The play cuts between past and present and explores how Eva's identity changes as she grows up in her English home. Eva, who changes her name to Evelyn to hide her past and her Jewish roots, is forced to confront painful memories when as an adult and a mother herself, her teenage daughter discovers old letters long since hidden away.

This extract is taken from the opening scene (Act 1, Scene 1) of the play. The action takes place in an attic or storage room of a house in London. One side of the stage represents Germany in 1938 and Helga is preparing her daughter Eva for her forthcoming journey to England on the *Kindertransport*. On the other side of the stage, Evelyn (who is Eva as an adult) is helping her daughter Faith choose some household objects for her impending move into her own flat. Both pairs of characters are separated by time as the action cuts between them. The printed extract here focuses solely on Eva and Helga's dialogue.

Ratcatcher music.

Dusty storage room filled with crates, bags, boxes and some old furniture.

Eva, dressed in clothes of the late 1930s, is sitting on the floor, reading. The book is a large, hard-backed children's storybook entitled Der Rattenfänger.

Helga, holding a coat, button, needle and thread, is nearby. She is well turned-out in clothes of the late 1930s.

Eva: What's an abyss, Mutti?

Helga: (*sitting down and ushering* Eva *to sit next to her*). An abyss is a deep and terrible chasm.

Eva: What's a chasm?

Helga: A huge gash in the rocks.

Eva: What's a . . .

Eva puts down the book. Music stops.

Helga: Eva, sew on your buttons now. Show me that you can do it.

Eva: I can't get the thread through the needle. It's too thick. You do it.

Helga: Lick the thread . . .

Eva: Do I have to?

Helga: Yes. Lick the thread.

Eva: I don't want to sew.

Helga: How else will the buttons get onto the coat?

Eva: The coat's too big for me.

Helga: It's to last next winter too.

Eva: Please.

Helga: No.

Eva: Why won't you help me?

Helga: You have to be able to manage on your own.

Eva: Why?

Helga: Because you do. Now, lick the thread.

Eva licks the thread.

Helga: That should flatten it . . . And hold the needle firmly and place the end of the thread between your fingers . . . not too near . . . that's it . . . now try to push it through.

Eva concentrates on the needle and thread.

Helga watches.

Helga: See. You don't need me. It's good.

Eva: I don't mind having my coat open a bit. Really. I've got enough buttons.

Helga: You'll miss it when the wind blows.

Eva:	Can't I do it later.
Helga:	There's no 'later' left, Eva.
Eva:	After the packing, after my story . . .
Helga:	Now.

Eva gives in and sews.

Eva:	(*sewing*) Why aren't Karla and Heinrich going on one of the trains?
Helga:	Their parents couldn't get them places.
Eva:	Karla said it's because they didn't want to send them away.
Helga:	Karla says a lot of silly things.
Eva:	Why's that silly?
Helga:	Of course they would send them away if they had places. Any good parent would do that.
Eva:	Why?
Helga:	Because any good parent would want to protect their child.
Eva:	Can't you and Vati protect me?
Helga:	Only by sending you away.
Eva:	Why will I be safer with strangers?
Helga:	Your English family will be kind.
Eva:	But they don't know me.
Helga:	Eva. This is for the best.
Eva:	Will you miss me?
Helga:	Of course, I will.
Eva:	Will you write to me?
Helga:	I've told you. I will do more than miss you and write to you. Vati and I will come. We will not let you leave us behind for very long. Do you think we would really let you go if we thought that we would never see you again?
Eva:	How long will it be before you come?
Helga:	Only a month or two. When the silly permits are ready.
Eva:	Silly permits.
Helga:	Silly, silly permits.
Eva:	The needle's stuck.

Helga, with difficulty, pulls the needle through.

Eva:	Finish it off for me.
Helga:	(*handing the sewing back to* Eva) No.

Eva takes the coat and carries on sewing.

Helga:	Try to meet other Jews in England.
Eva:	I will.
Helga:	They don't mind Jews there. It's like it was here when I was younger. It'll be good.

Eva: When you come, will Vati get his proper job back like he used to have?

Helga: I'm sure he will.

Eva: (*finishes sewing*) Finished.

Helga: Now let me check the case.

Helga picks up a case hidden amongst the boxes and opens and checks through it. Eva watches her.

Helga: (*pulling out a dress*) This suits you so well.

Eva: I'll only wear it for best. Promise.

Helga: (*re-folding the dress*) Someone will have to press out the creases when you get there.

Helga pulls a mouth organ out of the case.

Helga: What's this doing in here?

Eva: That's my mouth organ.

Helga: You're not allowed to take anything other than clothes.

Eva: But it was my last birthday present and I'm just beginning to get the tunes right.

Helga: The border guards will send you back to us if they find you with this. Then where will you be?

Eva: I'm sorry.

Helga gives the mouth organ to Eva and sets to reorganizing the case contents.

Kindertransport

As a group, read through the script then, in pairs, take the script away and read through the text before returning to the group to discuss their findings, or, with more confident readers, go 'around the class' with each student taking the next character's line.

Once the students have had an opportunity to read the text, lead a discussion addressing the following questions:

- How old do they think Eva is?
- Why does Helga insist on making Eva finish sewing the button on her coat? Why is being independent so important?
- Why do they think the coat must last two winters?
- When Helga speaks of coming to fetch Eva from England, do they think she means it? Do they think the permits Helga talks about really exist?
- Why is the mouth organ so important to Eva?
- What is the theatrical style of the play? How far do they agree it is written to represent 'real life' – one of the features of naturalistic drama?

Finally, ask the students what each character in turn is *trying to achieve* in the scene. This links with Stanislavski's idea of the *objective*, and it can change a number of times in a scene and during the course of a whole play.

Stage five

Before the group have a chance to work with sections of the script, it may be useful to use *hot-seating* to help build their understanding of characters in the play.

Hot-seating is a popular classroom drama convention in which the class members question or interview a fellow group member – or teacher – in role, who responds in the first person. Hot-seating can be useful within a drama to establish additional information about a particular character, for instance, the ideas, beliefs and attitudes that they might hold. Actors preparing for performance can use hot-seating as an opportunity to build up an imaginative history of the character, and can also experiment with the character's voice, movements and mannerisms or gestures during the interview.

One of the pitfalls of hot-seating is that it is difficult to sustain, and as it depends on the quality of the questions asked, can sometimes become trivial. It is useful when working with younger or inexperienced groups to keep control of the pace and tension necessary to sustain the work by taking the hot-seat yourself; or, as in the example in this unit, by 'choreographing' events beforehand.

The hot-seating exercise can be attempted first as a whole group, with two volunteers taking on the role of Eva and Helga being interviewed separately. Once this whole group task has been completed, place the students into smaller groups of five, with volunteers taking on the two roles while the other students ask the questions. Remind them that each character should be hot-seated separately.

Once the groups have had a chance to complete the task, share some of the improvisations. Was this a useful exercise to gain insight into the feelings and attitudes of the characters? Were there any similar responses, thoughts or ideas expressed in different groups?

Stage six

Now, return to the script and ask the students to work in pairs. (If working on the whole extract seems too daunting or time consuming, divide the class into groups of six, then ask them to sub-divide the extract into three sections. Each pair prepares their section, before joining the sections together for performance.) Tell the class that although both characters are female, boys can portray the roles as males and do not need to change the names of the characters.

Allow working time – 10 minutes or so – and introduce the following:

We discussed ideas of what each character is trying to achieve in the scene in an earlier discussion. In naturalistic drama, when actors develop their characters during rehearsal, one of the things they often consider is what the character is trying to achieve in the scene and in the play as a whole. This is the character's **objective***, and it influences how the scene is to be played and how characters speak and react to each other.*

The objective can be very simple, like 'I want Eva to finish her sewing,' or 'I want to reassure Eva everything will be alright,' but it must exist within the **given circumstances** *of the play. The given circumstances are the facts of the play that cannot be changed, such as time, location and action. Now quickly identify for yourself what you think your character's objective is in the section you are working on.*

If you think it might help, ask the students to annotate their script with their objective statements; *I want to . . .*

Allow time for the groups to prepare their work, and rehearse how they will stage running the sections together, before identifying a performance area and asking each group to share their scenes.

Once all the groups have presented, discuss each performance. Can the audience identify some of the different objectives the characters had? How did the actors show these objectives through their voice, movement and gesture?

Character objectives and motivation

We are touching here on the work of theatre director and actor Konstantin Stanislavsky (1863–1938), who over the course of many years developed his ideas into a unified 'system' for training actors. Stanislavsky's determination to take acting seriously, and to search for psychological realism and 'truth' led him to emphasize the 'inner life' of the character, asking actors to analyze their roles in detail. His work became very influential, and today many of his ideas about acting are taken for granted. The extent of the ubiquitous influence of Stanislavskian ideas can be evidenced in drama classrooms where inexperienced students sometimes equate *verisimilitude* with quality – in other words, acting which does not attempt to recreate 'real life' is often regarded as inferior!

One of Stanislavsky's key ideas is that characters in a play are constrained by the *given circumstances* of their context, and that identifying those constraints can help actors find believable behaviour and the ultimate – if paradoxical – aim: truthful acting!

His advice that actors should also identify their characters' *motivation* in a scene, and that this would provide a logical guide to the way that the character should relate to others, has also become commonplace in the rehearsal room and drama studio.

In the classroom notions like this can clearly be helpful to students in developing characters in their own scripted or improvised dramas. However, the notion of a 'well-rounded' character – and the other familiar precepts of naturalism – are relatively recent ideas in the history of drama, and the psychological emphasis of the 'system', strictly speaking, limits its use to realistic drama. Attempts to apply these ideas to highly stylized theatre – physical theatre, for instance – will run into problems!

Naturalistic acting is in fact very complex – and most young people find it challenging, particularly when asked to play characters considerably older than themselves – which is not unusual in school contexts. For this reason, many drama teachers prefer to work in more abstract, ensemble styles, which tend to be more inclusive and collaborative, and can produce high quality performances with relatively inexperienced groups.

One of the interesting problems caused by the assumption that psychological realism is the *holy grail* of acting can be seen in some assessment schemes for drama – where the highest levels of achievement can only be gained through demonstrating complex characters.

Stage seven

As a way of completing this section of the work and reminding the students that these are real events affecting real people, project or hand out the photograph of the girl on the ship from the photograph album exercise. Ask them to count the number of buttons on her coat.

For the next part of the work, tell the group that they will be working by themselves and distribute paper and pens. Ask the students to sit in a space on their own and remind them of the story in section one, stage one of the unit with which we began: what did the parents put in the children's suitcases and why did they do it?

Explain to the class that there were strict rules about what the *Kind* could take with them on the transport. First, the children were only allowed one bag or suitcase. Valuables, jewellery and musical instruments were not allowed. They were only allowed to take a small amount of cash, 10 Reichsmarks (the equivalent of about £35 today).

Families faced with packing their children's cases might have agonized over what to include; as well as practical items like clothes, many parents wanted their children to have something to remind them of home.

Read out the following accounts:

The authorities allowed the children to take only a small suitcase with them, so I could only take one of my dolls.

Marion Charles – a nine-year-old living in Berlin.[4]

I think that in all cases it was a very difficult thing for people to decide what things they might put into their small suitcase or bag. I still have here a silver spoon. My parents decided that I should have something to remind me of home. They perhaps knew the probability of us meeting again was very small and they had a knife, fork and spoon engraved with my name, Robert, and this is what remains. But consider the problem. How do you as a young person, how do you as a parent, decide what to put in one small case or bag? Do you put in things to do with washing and cleaning? Do you put in clothes? Toys? Do you put in mementoes of home maybe? What do you exclude? It's a great problem, and it was a great problem for all of us. I think that at the finish it was mostly clothing.

Source unknown

Ask the students to imagine they are faced with this dilemma. In the following exercise, they have a choice of roles: they can either take on the role of a child who is deciding for themselves the special thing they are to pack, or a parent choosing a keep sake to put in the suitcase for their child. Remind the students that the object need not have a great deal of monetary value, but should have emotional significance and attachment. Tell them that along with the object, they need to invent a brief history that goes with it that explains why it is significant.

Once the students have decided on their role and the object, ask them to draw a quick sketch of it with as much detail as possible on the paper you have provided. Allow a few minutes to complete their drawing before asking them to add a title that will help explain the significance of the object; if there was a label attached, what might it read?

- *A silver locket with a secret inside ...*
- *My mother's silk scarf with her name embroidered ...*
- *My favourite teddy who will look after me ...*
- *The key to our front door for your return ...*

Ask the students to stand up without talking and place their drawing on the floor in front of them. Tell them they now have the chance to walk around the space and look at the drawn objects of their classmates, and that they should do this quietly and without commenting or talking. Once they have had a chance to see all the other drawings, they should return to their own work and stand or sit quietly.

Collect in the drawings and keep them safe, as these will be used later in the drama.

Development – art and design

This exercise may provide you with ideas of how you could take the drawings of the objects from the drama, and develop them further by experimenting with different art techniques.

3D Construction

You could quite easily turn your sketch into a 3D model for an 'exhibition' of *Kindertransport* mementos. You do not have to attempt to create your models to scale; if your original drawing was of something really small like a locket or a ring, make your model much larger.

There are a number of ways of creating your piece of artwork: construction paper, cardboard and tape can be used to create the solid shape, and then the outside shell can be built up using glued parcel tape, or squares of newspaper, with a 2:1 PVA glue to water mix.

Once you are happy with the final shape, allow it to dry. At this stage, experiment with adding the language of the caption you included in your original drawing using pen and ink. The object could then be finished with a wash of colour and a final coat of PVA and water mix to seal it.

Other materials, such as wire and mesh covered with Mod Roc or a similar plaster of Paris product, fired clay or air drying paper clay, could also be used. You can make a cast by covering an object you wish to replicate with cling film. Then, use PVA glue and water mix with small squares of tissue paper to build up three to four layers all around the object. Once dried, carefully cut a slit in the cast from top to bottom that will allow you to remove the original object. Then paste more PVA and tissue paper on the seam to seal it up.

Lino cut prints

Turning your drawings into lino cut or 'press-on' prints can be extremely effective if the prints are displayed in the form of a wall hanging with each square representing a different object. If printing onto paper or card, these can be mounted onto a backing sheet, or 'stitched' together using string or ribbon to form a wall hanging. You will need help with the cutting tools and your teacher will give you either polystyrene tiles or lino to work with. Don't forget your prints can be applied onto fabric and displayed, or could be used to make a *patchwork quilt* of different squares of fabric.

Stage seven

Hand out the following extract from Diane Samuel's *Kindertransport* in which Helga gives her daughter Eva her 'travelling gift' of a pair of shoes, in which she has had some valuables hidden.

Helga:	Put the heel of the right shoe to your ear.
Eva:	Why?
Helga:	Do it.

Eva puts the heel to her ear.

Helga:	What can you hear?
Eva:	It sounds like . . .
Helga:	Yes?
Eva:	Ticking.
Helga:	My gold watch is in there.
Eva:	How?
Helga:	The cobbler did it.
Eva:	I'll look after it for you.
Helga:	And in the other heel are two rings, a chain with a Star of David and a charm bracelet for you. All made of gold.
Eva:	For me?
Helga:	From my jewellery box. A travelling gift.
Eva:	Thank you.
Helga:	My grandfather used to wear a black hat and coat. 'You are my children. You are my jewels.' He told me. 'We old ones invest our future in you.'

Eva hugs Helga.

Kindertransport

After reading through the script discuss the following:

- Why has Helga taken pains to hide her gold watch and jewellery in the heels of Eva's shoes?
- Do you think Eva understands the significance of the gift?
- Why do you think Helga talks about 'investing our future' in the children?

In reality, Helga would have been lucky to have anything of value left to give to her daughter. By 1939 in Germany and Austria, many Jewish people had already given up their homes, businesses, money and valuables to the state and after Kristallnacht, Jewish people were unfairly fined 1 billion Reichsmarks to pay for the damage caused by the anti-Semitic protests.

In pairs, the students should prepare the extract for performance. Even though the scene is short, the students might like to focus on highlighting the contrasting emotions of the two characters. Eva is surprised and delighted with her strange gift, Helga is perhaps more thoughtful and understandably more serious.

What do the students think the gifts represent for Helga?

Section two – leaving, the journey and arriving

Stage one

Explain that in this section of the work, the group will be working together to create one large dramatic sequence that is divided up into three distinct shorter scenes. Each scene will dramatize the moment of leaving, aspects of the journey and arrival in England.

It might be useful to divide the class up into three large groups and assign them their scene focus at this point. As well as providing the resource sheets, you will need to support each group as they prepare their work. The first task for each group is to read through their resource sheets, as these provide eyewitness accounts and historical information as well as identifying the theatrical approach the group should take to dramatize their work.

The Kindertransport was fairly well documented and a careful search of the Internet will reveal numerous sites that contain some very poignant photographs and telling accounts of the children at various stages of their journeys.

Leaving – group devising resource sheet

Nearly all the children on the *Kindertransport* travelled by special trains that were scheduled to take the children across the border to Holland, and from there by ship to England. There must have been an incredible sense of urgency to take advantage of the chance to escape, and a fear that the chance might be snatched away at the last minute.

Read the following accounts from eyewitnesses at the time.

The first party of children today left Prague . . . Here for 1½ hours there was a mixture of complete chaos, high excitement and passionate adieus . . . I did not see one of the kids crying. They were far too excited.[5]

. . . I saw my father coming to me, wanting to kiss me goodbye one last time. I leaned out of the window, about to kiss and stroke his face once more, when a group of SS men with large dogs and truncheons strode up to the train and pushed him and the other parents away from the train.

My father stumbled and a lady fell. I stayed as strong as I could, took one last look at my father as the platform receded, and prayed that I would see him and my mother again soon.[6]

One of the last memories before leaving home forever with the Children's Transport is of my father taking me aside and placing his hands on my head speaking the ancient Hebrew blessing asking God to protect and keep me safe.[7]

The authorities soon realized that they needed to avoid such emotional and highly charged scenes being played out in public, so ordered that families said their goodbyes in specially designated rooms. Older children, who might have realized how serious the situation was, were encouraged to look after the younger ones while parents tried to be strong for their children's sake.

You will be creating a piece of drama that is a montage of movement and sound. Imagine a busy railway platform. As well as the parents helping the children to get onto the train and saying their goodbyes, railway workers, officials and other passengers are all looking on. Choose one or two people to work with, before shaping a still image that is your contribution to the larger group picture. Each pair or three should now develop around 30 seconds of movement and language that starts with their still image and ends in a different still image. Once these sections have been devised, find a way of presenting your scene so that each short improvisation follows the next. A simple way of ensuring your drama is organized is making sure everyone is still until it is their turn to perform – although you might wish to experiment with more complicated ways of joining the short improvisation together, perhaps by using a repeated or shared phrase or gesture or using slow-motion instead of stillness.

The journey – group devising resource sheet

Nearly all the children on the *Kindertransport* travelled by special trains that were scheduled to take the children across the border to Holland, and from there by ship to England. There are accounts of the *Gestapo* insisting that the railway carriage windows were sealed shut and often the children's bags were searched for money and valuables. Once the trains had passed into Holland, there was a feeling of having escaped and the sense of relief must have been immense.

At last when I could no longer doubt that I had escaped I sent a thanksgiving to Heaven, and I could hardly help crying like a little child. (15-year-old boy)

The relief getting to Holland was immediate, you felt different in a free country, the ladies came on the trains and they gave us sweets and drinks and food, it was a wonderful thing. Only then did we realize the oppression we'd left behind, you don't realize what you're missing when you haven't got freedom.[8]

The children passed the time chatting, perhaps playing cards and the musical instruments they had taken against the rules. Sandwiches were unpacked and eaten and some of the older children looked after their younger brothers and sisters as well as any younger unaccompanied children. There were a few adults who went with each transport; they were trusted to return to Germany once the children had arrived safely in England.

Divide your large group into two smaller groups. Each group will represent one crowded train carriage over the course of several hours. You are going to create three separate images that attempt to capture the different phases of the journey.

The first is EXCITEMENT, the second is EXHAUSTION and the third is RELIEF.

You will have to create the three images that go with each title. Think about how you can include contrasts in facial expression, body shape and levels for each image. You will have to practise moving from one image to the next smoothly and efficiently. These transitions are very much part of the stylized drama; experiment with slow-motion and making the movements very precise and definite. Finally, once you have the images and the transitions rehearsed, practise them in a cycle by repeating the sequence three times. As there is no speech in your piece, your teacher will play some music when you perform your piece.

Arriving – group devising resource sheet

Nearly all the children on the *Kindertransport* travelled by special trains that were scheduled to take the children across the border to Holland, and from there by ship to England. On arrival at Harwich or Southampton, *Refugee Child Movement* officials would board the ship and place a card around each child's neck with an identifying number. From there the children would have their papers stamped by a medical officer and an immigration official. The children could then pass through customs.

Children that had an assigned family were put on a train to Liverpool Street Station in London and from there embarked on their new life with their host families. Children that did not have a 'guarantor' to take them in were sent to summer holiday camps at Dovercourt, near to Harwich.

The children would have been tired and anxious after their journey but excited to see the English coastline. The arrival of the Kind was well documented at the time. Using the Internet, search for images of Kindertransport children arriving in Harwich. If you cannot do this, imagine a photograph of the children waving from the ship as it arrives in port. Now, imagine if the photograph was reversed and you could see the people behind the camera on the dock, what would they make of the group of foreign children waving at them from on board the ship?

Split your group into two. One group will be the children waving from the ship; the other group will be the people standing on the dock. They could be sailors or dockworkers, officials of the Refugee Children Movement (RCM), police officers, passengers from other ships or perhaps families there to welcome the children.

Arrange yourselves to create the two 'sides' of the imaginary photograph as a still image. Each student should have their own pose and position. As soon as you have created both sides of the still image, each member of the group has to devise two or three lines to be said in character that capture the feelings of the children or their hopes and fears for the future. Remember many of them would not speak any English, they had left behind their families with just what they could carry and they did not know where they were going. It must have been quite overwhelming.

You will need to find a way for each character to say their few lines. This can be done as a 'step-out' with each person stepping out of the still image to speak their words. You might wish to explore using movement and mine instead of a still image. Experiment with slow motion or a repeated gesture to capture the mood and atmosphere of the scene.

These improvisations will need around 20 minutes to prepare. Once the groups are happy with their work, arrange the space so that they can be performed in sequence. By playing some atmospheric instrumental music, you will be able to enhance the dramatic action considerably and make the transitions between the scenes more theatrical.

Once the work has been performed, evaluate the drama by discussing some of the techniques being used.

● Was the stylized – or abstract – drama useful in communicating meaning, mood and narrative?

Kindertransport

- If they had more time, what else might they have added?
- Would this work help if they were devising a whole play based on the *Kindertransport*?
- Did the work accurately capture or reflect the experience of the real life *Kind*?

Stage two – the first meeting

> *I was homesick, fiercely loyal to my parents and determined to do things their way, not the English way. I had no wish to become a nice little English girl, which was Auntie's ambition for me. At the time my attitude seemed to me entirely reasonable; in retrospect I must have been a trying child.*[9]

Ask the students to imagine the emotions the *Kindertransport* children might have felt on meeting their host families for the first time. Now ask them the same question from the host family's point of view. Are there any similarities? Remind them that one of the problems might have been the language barrier – not all of the displaced children would have been able to speak English or the host families been able to speak German, Austrian or Czech.

In pairs, ask the students to create a short improvisation that explores the moment a *Kindertransport* child is met by the mother or father of the host family they are to be staying with for the first time. This meeting would often take place in the waiting room of Liverpool Street Station in London. Is there any tension in the first meeting? How do they greet each other? Ask them to consider how to show any language barrier that might have existed, perhaps by using any German vocabulary or language they might know. They could theatrically express this problem by using English words, but having each character saying they do not understand the other:

Child: My suitcase is so heavy, do we have far to go?
Mother: I'm sorry love, I don't understand a word ... that suitcase looks heavy, can you pick it up?

The improvisation should end with the pair leaving the waiting room for the next stage of their journey.

Share the work in the following manner: place the pairs into two 'teams' facing each other. Ask the pairs in the group performing first to find a place in the performing area and create a still image that is the start of their improvisation. Each pair then shares their work in order, finishing with a still image that signals the next pair to start. Share both large groups work and evaluate the drama.

Hand out the third extract from *Kindertransport* by Diane Samuels. Explain that in this episode, Eva meets Lil for the first time at the train station. Lil has been delayed and Eva gets her English muddled up as she sees Lil for the first time.

Eva: (*standing up*) Goodbye to you.

Lil: (*to Eva*) Poor lamb. You must be exhausted. Scared as well probably. Last thing you need is me being late.

Eva stands and bows.

Eva: Goodbye to you.

Lil: Goodbye?

Eva: Goodbye.

Lil: Who taught you English? German teacher was it? (*Holds out her hand.*) Hello.

Eva holds out her hand.

Lil: (*shaking Eva's hand*) Hello.

Eva: (*carefully*) Hello.

Lil: (*speaking slowly*) My name is Mrs Miller. Lil Miller.

Eva: Angenehm. (*I'm pleased to meet you.*)

Lil: I'm sorry, love. Don't speak German. You'll have to learn English.

Points to Eva's case and gestures 'out'.

Set to go then?

Eva picks up her case puts on her coat, and stands ready.

Lil: (*pointing at the label with the number and the Star of David on it*) What's this?

Eva: Ich much es tragen. Ich hasse es. (*I had to wear it. I hate it.*)

Lil: Why don't we get rid of it?

Eva hesitates.

Lil: You don't need it on now I've come.

Eva: Und wenn ich meine Nummer vergesse? (*What if I forget my number?*)

Lil takes the label off.

Lil: All gone.

Eva: Sind sie sicher? (*Can you do that?*)

Lil: (*gesturing*) Over. Finished. Done. Goodbye. Yes. That's the word. Goodbye.

Eva: Ich verstehe. (*I understand.*)

Lil takes her hand.

Lil: I like you. Come on. D'you like singing?

Kindertransport

How does this script compare with the students' own interpretations?

Working in the same pairs, ask the students to stage the text excerpt, observing the stage directions carefully. (The English translations in brackets are for information and should not be spoken.) Ask the students to focus on the physicality of the characters. Is Eva attempting to be quite formal and polite as she greets Lil, despite getting her English wrong? The moment Lil takes off Eva's label that she has been wearing round her neck seems significant, how can the students mark that significance?

This exercise will give you the opportunity to do some creative 'in-role' writing.

Task: before the start of the war in 1939, the *Kind* and their parents were able to write to each other, although as the situation deteriorated for the parents, this might have become difficult or impossible. Do some research and see if you can find any real examples of correspondence in historical archives. Visit the Moving Here website http://www.movinghere.org.uk and the Weiner Library website: http://www.wienerlibrary.co.uk, both have sections on the *Kindertransport* and accounts from both parents and their children.

What sort of things do you think a parent might write in their first letter to their son or daughter in England? Don't forget they might not wish their child to worry, so perhaps they do not go into detail about what is happening at home. In reality, the threat of being deported to the concentration camps must have been ever present in the parents' minds. Do you think the parent might ask questions about the host family and their home? Perhaps they might remind their child to always be polite, make friends, do well at school and practise their English.

The son or daughter's first letter might be full of descriptions about their strange new surroundings. An event like going on a London red double-decker bus, the different and unfamiliar foods and drinks, the welcome from the host family and the first day at school could all be things they might write about. Older *Kind* might also be aware of the danger their parents faced, and in fact many tried in vain to arrange a job for their parents so they could get a visa and join them in the UK.

Write two letters, one from the point of view of the child and one from the parent. The letters could be replies to each other or they could have 'crossed' in the post. Think about how you can lay your letters out – and you might like to consider how to age the letters slightly to give the appearance of a document that is over 70 years old. Soaking the letter in a shallow dish of cooled strong tea before carefully drying it out will add an effective aged appearance!

Stage three – final reflective phase

Saw a poodle in a jacket fastened with a pin,

Saw a door opened and a cat let in:

But they weren't German Jews, my dear, but they weren't German Jews.

W. H. Auden, Refugee Blues (1939)[10]

In 1939, Europe was on the brink of war and people were suspicious of strangers and refugees. Countries including Great Britain were reluctant to accept any Jewish refugees, and after the horror of *Kristallnacht* the helping hand of the *Kindertransport* was only extended to children and not their parents or relatives.

> *'There are now two sorts of countries in the world, those that want to expel the Jews and those that don't want to admit them.'*
>
> Chaim Weizmann – First President of the State of Israel: testimony given at the Peel Commission, Jerusalem, 1936

Around 50 per cent of the *Kindertransport* children were placed with host families. Initially the organizers attempted to find Jewish families for the children to live with, but as numbers grew this became more challenging. The other *Kind,* without host families to live with, were housed in reception camps, hostels or agricultural training farms in the country.

Despite the dreadful circumstances in which the children had left their homes, the majority of children had a very positive experience with families that were patient and loving. Arriving in England was the start of a longer journey as the children attempted to adjust to life in a foreign country. For many, they would become the sole survivors of their family, as their birth parents, relatives and friends were murdered in the Holocaust.

Explain that there is a memorial to the *Kindertransport* children in Liverpool Street Station. Created by Frank Meisler, it shows a group of *Kind* with their cases. Sixteen brass plaques are inscribed with the names of the cities from which the children travelled. Inside the station, another sculpture by Flor Kent features original objects that were brought by the children, arranged in a large glass suitcase.

As a final, reflective task distribute the drawings of the objects the students created when they completed the case packing task. In groups of five tell them they are to create their own version of a memorial to the children of the *Kindertransport*.

Read out or project the Robert Browning poem, *The Pied Piper of Hamelin: A Child's Story* (1888).

Out came the children running.

All the little boys and girls,

With rosy cheeks and flaxen curls,

And sparkling eyes and teeth like pearls,

Tripping and skipping, ran merrily after

The wonderful music with shouting and laughter.

Kindertransport

Explain that they are to create a display of the objects on the floor. Each student then sits or stands next to the object that they drew. Ask them to imagine that each of the objects has an 'echo' that crosses time – and the title or label they added to their drawing will form the language of that echo in the drama.

For the performance they should attempt to read out the title or label in role as their character at the time of giving or packing the case. They should add a simple mimed action – perhaps that of using or holding the object, or carefully packing it in the case. To make the drama as effective as possible, there should be no other comments or discussion from the group as each student performs. Tell the groups that they can use any lines from the Robert Browning poem to start, end, or link their drama together.

Encouraging the students to experiment with different vocal and movement qualities, and repeating the language and movement in a cyclic pattern will give an abstract quality to the work, which may add significance and meaning. When the work is shared, allowing students to choose suitable music to underscore the drama will also add mood and atmosphere. Some students may wish to develop their brief title into a longer monologue, giving more confident or older students the opportunity to explore characterization in terms of voice, movement and gesture.

The resources for this Unit are available for download at www.routledge.com/9780415572064

Notes

Introduction

1 Countesthorpe College in Leicestershire, which, during its first phase (1970–76) was run democratically by a combined staff–student body and introduced many 'progressive' innovations including a non-coercive, individualized curriculum and a team-led 'schools within schools, structure': 'arguable the most remarkable example of co-constructed curriculum we have ever had in secondary schools in England' (Fielding in Halstead and Hayden (2008). See also Watts (1977)).

2 Wigan LEA, which, during the 1970s and 1980s, promoted an innovative entitlement curriculum model based on areas of experience rather than subjects.

3 In 1904 the (English) Government's Board of Education published the first of its annual Regulations for Secondary Schools, defining a four year subject-based course leading to a certificate in *English language and literature, geography, history*, a *foreign language, mathematics, science, drawing, manual work, physical training*, and, for girls, *housewifery*. Gillard (2011)

4 *Dangerously Irrelevant* is the title of the educational online 'blog' of Dr Scott McLeod: http://bigthink.com/blogs/dangerously-irrelevant

5 As one commentator puts it: 'Today's kindergarteners will be retiring in the year 2067. We have no idea of what the world will look in five years, much less 60 years, yet we are charged with preparing our students for life in that world. Our students are facing many emerging issues such as global warming, famine, poverty, health issues, a global population explosion and other environmental and social issues. These issues lead to a need for students to be able to communicate, function and create change personally, socially, economically and politically on local, national and global levels', at
http://www.21stCenturySchools.com/What_is_21st_Century_Education.htm

6 Schell (2000), p. 11.

7 McMahon (1997).

8 http://www.thersa.org/projects/education/opening-minds The five key competences around which *Opening Minds* are based do provide a useful framework for organizing

185

learning: the teaching units in this book clearly contribute to the development of the five competences; however we found them rather broad, and when 'auditing' the units found that we were 'addressing' most of them, most of the time!

9 http://studioschoolstrust.org/studio-schools

10 http://www.wholeeducation.org/

11 http://www.campaign-for-learning.org.uk/cfl/index.asp

12 Donovan *et al.* (1999); Newman and Associates (1996); Newmann *et al.* (1995); Nolan and Francis (1992), cited in Mims (2003).

13 Marra (2010).

14 Ibid.

15 A term coined by Mark Prensky in his book, *Digital Natives, Digital Immigrants* (2001).

16 For example, Essa Academy in Bolton, UK, introduced from 2009 a bespoke wireless network system and provided each pupil and teacher with a hand-held touchscreen device in order to stimulate 'anytime, anywhere learning'.

17 Schell (2000).

18 Carroll, Anderson and Cameron (2006).

19 Dettori (2007).

20 The title of a book by Jonathan Neelands (1992).

21 See O'Neill and Johnson (1984).

22 A six-year-old student having been involved in a *Mantle of the Expert* drama – cited at http://www.mantleoftheexpert.com

23 Dorothy Heathcote and Gavin Bolton provide some interesting, but sometimes complex, examples of MOE in their 1995 book *Drama for Learning*. These ideas have since been taken up and developed through the website http://www.mantleoftheexpert.com

24 As in the 'English Baccalaureate' introduced by the UK Coalition Government Education Minister Michael Gove in 2011, where school league tables are based upon the number of students in each school achieving a grade 'C' or above in their GCSE examinations in five subjects: English, Mathematics, Science, History (or Geography) and a Foreign or Ancient language.

25 Eisner writes convincingly about the validity of *expressive objectives* in arts education – learning which may be unpredictable, encourages diversity and may be acquired through rich engagement with an arts process, as distinct from *instructional objectives* which 'emphasise the acquisition of the known … in a predictive model of curriculum development' Eisner (1967).

26 Wolf *et al.* (1991).

27 Adapted from Mueller (undated).

28 Lombardy (2007).

29 As promoted by the UK Blair Government's 'National Strategy' for education, http://nationalstrategies.standards.dcsf.gov.uk/primary/assessment/assessmentforlearningafl

30 Lombardy (2007).

31 In *Drama, Narrative and Moral Education* (1998), and *Drama, Literacy and Moral Education, 5–11* (2000).

32 Quoted by Wombles (2011).

33 Perhaps the most notable critic taking this line was history teacher Chris McGovern who campaigned to change the content of history GCSE examinations in the late 1980s.

34 Critics cite perhaps apocryphal examples of students being asked to write empathetic accounts from the perspective of concentration camp guards.

35 Postmodern historians such as Keith Jenkins doubt the possibility of empathizing with people from the past. Interestingly, Jenkins' position also leads him to describe historians' output as *stories* – acknowledging that their own beliefs and motivations will mean that 'a work of history is as much about the historian's own worldview and ideological positions as it is about past events'. This is actually quite close to the way in which dramatists – and drama teachers – might fruitfully regard history!

36 As in this example taken from the University of East Anglia (UK) Post Graduate Certificate in Education history course website: 'Role Play and practical demonstration provide the entry ticket to the disco of history by arming pupils with an insight into concept, a sense of context, or an appreciation of ideas and attitudes of those in the past. Active involvement of the vast majority of the class is the key. Let's remember the words of Bruner: "Experience and do rather than transmit."'

1 Foundlings

1 Available online at http://www.gutenberg.org/files/19361/19361-h/19361-h.htm

2 See also pp. 34–35.

3 A 2010 exhibition at the Foundling Museum, Threads of Feeling, displaying eighteenth century fabric birth tokens, has an online slideshow of exhibits with music: http://www.threadsoffeeling.com. They also have a *Facebook* site with many high quality images of foundling tokens: http://www.facebook.com/media/set/fbx/?set=a.194796887222129.39725.142916505743501

2 Van Diemen's Land

1 We are indebted to the late Dr John Fines for providing the initial idea – and something of the working method – for parts of this drama.

3 Persuasion

1 See Introduction, pp. 5–6.

2 See Kagan (2001).

3 Published in 1995 by Heinemann.

4 Child labour

1 See also pp. 5, 50,51.
2 http://www.historyhome.co.uk/readings/watercre.htm
3 Letter to Mr Mann (11 December 1813): http://www.spartacus.schoolnet.co.uk/IRworkhouse.children.htm
4 http://www.spartacus.schoolnet.co.uk/IRblincoe.htm
5 http://www.spartacus.schoolnet.co.uk/IRscavengers.htm
6 On *Here's the Tender Coming* (2009) EMI CD 687 1222.
7 Older students may be interested to read a recent article by John Harris in the Guardian newspaper: *Where is the Protest Music for 2010?* – which also provides a link to a contemporary example – *The Agitator*, http://www.guardian.co.uk/music/2010/dec/14/agitator-protest-music-2010
8 http://www.unicef.org.uk/putitright
9 http://www.youtube.com/watch?v=OtnkBCqjZAI
10 http://www.guardian.co.uk/business/2007/oct/28/ethicalbusiness.india
11 Petition from child worker, Bangladesh, 1994: Stearman (1999).
12 Gardner (2008).

6 Eyam plague village

1 Samuel Pepys, 7 June 1665, http://www.pepys.info/1665/1665.html
2 http://www.gutenberg.org/files/376/376-h/376-h.htm
3 http://www.gutenberg.org/files/376/376-h/376-h.htm
4 http://www.gutenberg.org/files/376/376-h/376-h.htm
5 In *Structuring Drama Work* (1980).
6 Or 'existential mode'. See Bolton (1979).

7 Wordless books

1 Coe (1997).
2 http://bemberess.com/portfolio/assets/whitecollar/wc_book/whitecollar.htm
3 See Goffman (1974); Heathcote (1980).

8 The case of Lizzie Borden

1 We are grateful to Joy Sherlock and her students for sharing the teaching on which this unit is based.
2 Opie and Opie (1974).
3 Hoffman's *Strewwelpeter (Straw-headed Peter)* was translated for his children by Mark Twain in 1891 – a year before the equally grotesque Lizzie Borden events – although the official American translation was not published until the 1930s.

4 See p. 91.

5 See p. 132.

6 Most notably, the ubiquitous scene where cast members – representing characters from the protagonist's past life – circle around them whilst they sleep; tension builds through chanting, and the scene ends with a loud scream as the poor haunted person awakes!

7 https://lizzie-borden.com/storeFront/index.php

8 Websites like this may help: http://www.independent.co.uk/news/people/news/the-ten-most-notorious-female-criminals–1792598.html

9 Kindertransport

1 http://www.wienerlibrary.co.uk/wls/stories/kinder/settingupthetransports/organisation.aspx

2 http://www.annefrank.org

3 Published in 2008.

4 http://www.historylearningsite.co.uk/kindertransport.htm

5 Letter from Prague transport organization, http://www.wienerlibrary.co.uk/wls/stories/kinder/thejourney/sayinggoodbye.aspx

6 http://www.historylearningsite.co.uk/kindertransport.htm

7 http://www.wienerlibrary.co.uk/wls/stories/kinder/thejourney/sayinggoodbye.aspx

8 http://www.wienerlibrary.co.uk/wls/stories/kinder/thejourney/onthewaytobritain.aspx

9 http://www.wienerlibrary.co.uk/wls/stories/kinder/lifeintheuk/hostfamilies.aspx

10 http://www.poemhunter.com/poem/refugee-blues

Bibliography

Berona, D. A. (2008) *Wordless Books – The Original Graphic Novels*: Adams

Bolton, G. (1979) *Towards a Theory of Drama in Education*: Longman

Brecht, B. (1976) *The Caucasian Chalk Circle*: Heinemann

Carroll, J., Anderson, M. & Cameron, D. (2006) *Real Players? Drama, Technology and Education*: Trentham Books

Coe, M. (1997) *Red Shoes*: Good Stuff Press, http://www.graphicwitness.org/contemp/mandy.htm

Defoe, D. (2010) *A Diary of the Plague Year*: OUP

Dettori, G. (2007) 'Book Review', *British Journal of Educational Technology*, Vol. 38, Issue 5, pp. 953–4, September 2007

Edgar, D. and Dickens, C. (1982) *The Life and Adventures of Nicholas Nickleby*: Joseph Weinburger Plays

Edmundson, H. (based on the novel by Gavin, J.) (2005) *Coram Boy*: Nick Hern Books

Eisner, E. (1967) 'Expressive and Instructional Educational Objectives: Their Formulation and Use in Curriculum', *Instructional Objectives; AERA Monograph Series on Curriculum Evaluation No. 3*: Rand McNally

Faultley, M. and Savage, J. (2011) *Cross-curricular Teaching and Learning in the Secondary School: The Arts*: David Fulton

Foxton, D. (1994) *A Memory of Lizzie*, from *Sepia and Song* (anthology): Nelson Thornes Ltd

Frank, A. (2007) *The Diary of a Young Girl*: Puffin

Gardner, L. (2008) *1968: Year Zero for British Theatre*, The Guardian Theatre Blog, 19 June 2008, http://www.guardian.co.uk/stage/theatreblog/2008/jun/19/1968year zeroforbritishtheatre

Gavin, J. (2004) *Coram Boy*: Egmont Books Ltd

Gillard, D. (2011) *Education in England: A Brief History*, http://www.educationeng-land.org.uk/history

Goffman, E. (1974) *Frame Analysis*: Harper & Row

Halstead, M. and Hayden, G (eds) (2008) *The Common School and the Comprehensive Ideal*: Wiley-Blackwell

Heathcote, D. (1980) *Role Function and Frame Distance*, http://www.moeplanning. co.uk/wp-content/uploads/2008/04/frame-distance.pdf

Heathcote, D. and Bolton, G. (1995) *Drama for Learning*: Heinemann

Hoffman, H. (1845) *Der Struwwelpeter*, English edition (1995): Dover Publications Inc.

Hughes, R. (2003) *The Fatal Shore*: Vintage

Jocelyn, M. (2005) *A Home for Foundlings*: Tundra Books

Kagan, S. (2001) *Co-operative Learning*: Kagan Publishing

Lewis, M. and Rainer, J. (2005) *Teaching Classroom Drama and Theatre*: Routledge

Lewis, M. and Rainer, J. (2006) *GCSE Drama – book and CD ROM*: OUP

Lombardy, M. M. (2007) *Authentic Learning for the 21st Century: An Overview*: Educause Learning initiative Paper 1, May.

Marra, T. (2010) *Authentic Learning Environments*: University of Michigan, http:// www-personal.umich.edu/~tmarra/authenticity/page3.html

McMahon, M. (1997) *Social Constructivism and the World Wide Web – A Paradigm for Learning*: Paper presented at the ASCILITE conference, Perth, Australia

Mims, C. (2003) 'Authentic Learning: A Practical Introduction & Guide for Implementation', *Meridian: A Middle School Computer Technologies Journal*, Vol 6, Issue 1, http://www.ncsu.edu/meridian/win2003/authentic_learning/

Mitter, S. (1992) *Systems of Rehearsal: Stanislavsky, Brecht, Growtowski, Peter Brook*: Routledge

Mueller, J. (undated) *Authentic Assessment Toolbox*, http://jfmueller.faculty.noctrl. edu/toolbox/index.htm

Neelands, J. (1980) *Structuring Drama* Work, 2nd edn: CUP

Neelands, J. (1992) *Learning Through Imagined Experience*: Hodder & Stoughton

O'Neill, C. and Johnson, L. (eds) (1984) *Dorothy Heathcote – Collected Writings on Education and Drama*: Northwestern University Press

Opie, I. and Opie, P. (compilers) (1974) *The Classic Fairy Tales*: Oxford University Press

Prensky. M. (2001) 'Digital Natives, Digital Immigrants', *On the Horizon*, Vol. 9, No. 5, http://www.marcprensky.com/writing/prensky%20-%20digital%20natives,%20 digital%20immigrants%20-%20part1.pdf

Samuels, D. (2008) *Kindertransport*, 2nd edn: Nick Hern Books

Schell, J. W. (2000) 'Think About Authentic Learning and then Authentic Assessment', Using Authentic Assessment in Vocational Education Information Series No. 381: Ohio State University, http://www.calpro-online.org/eric/docs/custer/ custer3.pdf

Stanislavsky, C. (1989) *An Actor Prepares*: Routledge

Stearman, K. (1999) *Slavery Today*: Hodder Wayland

Taylor, D. (1996) *The Roses of Eyam*: Heinemann

Walker, G. (2007) *Graphic Witness – Four Wordless Graphic Novels*: Firefly

Watts, J. (1977) *The Countesthorpe Experience*: Allen & Unwin

Watts, J. (1980) *Towards an Open School*: Longman

Bibliography

Wedd, K. (2004) *The Foundling Museum Guidebook*: The Foundling Museum

Willett, J. (1977) *The Theatre of Bertolt Brecht*: Methuen

Winston, J. (1998) *Drama, Narrative and Moral Education*: Falmer

Winston, J. (2000) *Drama, Literacy and Moral Education, 5–11*: David Fulton

Wolf, D., Bixby, J., Glenn, J. and Gardner, H. (1991) 'To Use Their Minds Well: Investigating New Forms of Student Assessment', *Review of Research in Education*

Wombles, K. 'Through A Glass Darkly: PBS's Autism Now And Simon Baron-Cohen's The Science Of Evil', *Science 2.0*, 17 April 2011, http://www.science20.com/countering_tackling_woo_and_science_asds/through_glass_darkly_pbss_autism_now_and_simon_baroncohens_science_evil−78206

Web resources

Frank Meisler, Sculptor and *Kindertransport* child
http://www.frank-meisler.com/kindertransport.html

Moving Here, 200 years of Migration to England
http://www.movinghere.org.uk/

Through My Eyes: stories of conflict, belonging and identity
http://www.throughmyeyes.org.uk/

Imperial War Museum, London
http://www.iwm.org.uk/

Weiner Library Institute of Contemporary History, London
http://www.wienerlibrary.co.uk

History Learning Site
http://www.historylearningsite.co.uk/

Association of Jewish Refugees
http://www.ajr.org.uk/

Red Shoes, by Mandy Coe
http://www.graphicwitness.org/contemp/mandy.htm

Lizzie Borden
http://law2.umkc.edu/faculty/projects/ftrials/lizzieborden/bordenhome.html

Babes in the Wood
http://norfolkcoast.co.uk/myths/ml_babesinwood.htm

Phaeton
http://www.mythindex.com/greek-mythology/P/Phaethon.html
http://www.theoi.com/Titan/Phaethon.html

Van Diemen's Land
http://www.utas.edu.au/library/companion_to_tasmanian_history/F/Frontier%20
Conflict.htm

Foundlings
http://www.foundlingmuseum.org.uk/exhibit_temp.php